Praise for

Aesop &
the CEO

by David Noonan

"In *Aesop and the CEO*, author David Noonan shares fifty real-life and fabled examples that serve to illustrate just what it means to take ownership for your work. Whether you have two minutes or two hours, your investment in reading this book will be time well spent."

— **Joseph A. "Bud" Ahearn**
Vice Chairman, CH2M HILL

"I thoroughly enjoyed these engaging and unique insights. For those in business and/or management positions, *Aesop and the CEO* is a must read."

— **Timothy P. Cahill**
Massachusetts State Treasurer and
Author of *Profiles in the American
Dream: The Real-Life Stories of the
Struggles of American Entrepreneurs*

"*Aesop and the CEO* is a refreshing mix of timeless fables and modern business challenges, reminding us that the lessons do not change—only the protagonists do."

— **Tom Glocer**
CEO, Reuters Group PLC

"Just as Aesop's fables have come down to us through the ages, the business lessons presented here will surely stand the test of time, making *Aesop and the CEO* an excellent investment for every business reference library."

— **Anne G. Peach, R.N., M.S.N.**
COO, M. D. Anderson Cancer
Center (Orlando)

"*Aesop and the CEO* is a brilliant book, one of the best business books in recent memory. It contains the wisdom of the ages and should be read by every CEO and company president."

— **Alfred J. Roach**
Founder and Chairman of the
Board of TII Network
Technologies, Inc.

"*Aesop and the CEO* is a totally relaxed and enjoyable way to relearn powerful business strategies. My business and I will be forever grateful."

— **Edward Roemke**
President & CEO,
InsWorld.com, Inc.

Aesop &
the CEO

Powerful Business Insights
from Aesop's Ancient Fables

David C. Noonan

NELSON BOOKS
A Division of Thomas Nelson Publishers
Since 1798

www.thomasnelson.com

For Clare,
my loving wife,
who always believed.

Published in Nashville, Tennessee, by Thomas Nelson, Inc.

Library of Congress Cataloging-in-Publication Data

Noonan, David C.
    Aesop and the CEO : powerful business insights from Aesop's ancient fables / David C. Noonan.
      p. cm.
    Includes bibliographical references.
    ISBN 0-7852-6010-2 (hardcover)
    1. Leadership—Moral and ethical aspects. 2. Industrial management—Moral and ethical aspects.
3. Aesop's fables—Adaptations. I. Title.
HD57.7.N65 2005
174'.4—dc22   2004028344

Printed in the United States of America

05 06 07 08 09 QW 5 4 3 2 1

*Propose honest things, follow wholesome counsels,
and leave the event to God.*

—FROM AESOP'S LETTER TO HIS ADOPTED SON

Contents

Contents

WINNING BUSINESS STRATEGIES

HUMAN RESOURCES
(Conflict Resolution)

HUMAN RESOURCES
(Motivating and Inspiring)

Contents

NEGOTIATIONS, MERGERS, *and* ALLIANCES

Preface

The idea for this book came to me as I read a modern update of "The Ant and the Grasshopper" fable in a business travel magazine. I thought I was up to speed on the fables, thinking I knew just about all of them and believing them to be primarily short tales for children's bedtime. After some preliminary research, though, I learned that I didn't know most of the fables simply because there were more than two hundred of them in the public domain. Moreover, Aesop originally conceived and compiled the fables to instruct adults—not children—in proper and prudent behavior.

As a consultant to businesses and government for twenty-five years, I witnessed a lot of human interaction—good and bad. It seemed a logical step to take a fresh look at the fables, focusing on one or more of the business lessons embedded in each tale. I decided it would be a natural transition to move from Aesop's original life lessons to modern business lessons.

Why mix business and morals? An overwhelming majority of us believe in God. Can we separate our spiritual beliefs from our conduct at work? Can we suspend our moral codes of behavior once the Sabbath is over? We are obliged to live good *lives*. We can't have one set of morals for home and a different set for work.

I believe Aesop's short morality plays have an important place in today's business world. One needs only to pick up a newspaper or turn on the news to see how far many corporations have strayed from moral business practices and efficient management. Coca-Cola paid Burger King more than $20 million, admitting it rigged taste tests for its new frozen drink. Sony Pictures agreed to pay $326,000 to settle charges of deceptive advertising as a result of inventing fake critic David Manning and his glowing reviews of Sony films and attributing them to Connecticut's *Ridgefield Press*. Mitsubishi ordered an automobile recall, admitting to covering up car defects such as failing brakes, malfunctioning clutches, and fuel tanks prone to falling off. Publishers Clearing House announced an $18 million settlement as part of an agreement to curb allegedly deceptive sweepstakes promotions.

Bridgestone/Firestone Inc. and Ford Motor Company battled hundreds of personal injury lawsuits arising from rollover accidents involving the Ford Explorer and Firestone Wilderness tires. General Motors won a settlement from NBC, which confessed that its *Dateline* show rigged GM truck explosions in a segment using a hidden remote-control device. Top managers at Enron and WorldCom stand accused of defrauding investors, deceiving employees, and causing two of the largest bankruptcies in the history of American business. Citigroup, WorldCom's lead banker, agreed to pay $2.65 billion to investors, the second largest payment ever by a bank to settle a securities class-action lawsuit alleging fraud. Cendant Corporation retains the top spot with its payment of $2.85 billion in 2000.

The list goes on. The U.S. Air Force suspended Boeing Aircraft from bidding on future rocket contracts when it found out the company stole twenty-five thousand documents from Lockheed Martin when the two companies competed for a contract in 1998. More recently, Boeing finds itself accused of bypassing federal procurement laws when it struck a deal to lease one hundred Boeing 767s to the air force. Bank One, Bank of America, Alliance Capital, Janus, Putnam Investments, and Strong Mutual Funds are accused of late trading or market timing of their mutual funds to the detriment of common shareholders.

These are not fly-by-night companies in the news, but well-established and well-known firms with millions of stockholders and, in most cases, long-standing track records in business. What goes wrong? In some cases, it's merely the result of a few bad employees acting irresponsibly. But in others, the deception or fraud is a deliberate corporate decision sanctioned at the very top of a firm.

The world of business has changed enormously since Aesop's time, but people haven't. Now more than ever, there is a need for strong, ethical leadership and efficient management at every company level. Now more than ever, good people must step up and reaffirm that integrity, honesty, and goodness are as critical to a business's survival as a strong bottom line. So what better time than now in this post-Enron world to reintroduce the lessons taught by Aesop almost six hundred years before Christ?

To illuminate the business lessons on management, leadership, marketing, sales, human resources, hiring, firing, mergers, negotiations, and product development, I turned to the experts, men and women in industry and government, both living and dead, who have compiled impressive track records as dynamic leaders and managers in their particular fields of business or governance. I compiled a list of some of the best business books of all time written by or about these experts, realizing that such a list would be subject to debate and that every individual could compile his own list that could and would look different from mine. Nevertheless, I developed my list of best business books using a mix of the following criteria: those books with the greatest sales according to *Publishers Weekly*, those that have been identified by the business world as seminal or groundbreaking, and those recommended by business schools and *BusinessWeek* as essential for a complete business library. I graciously concede that the list is not necessarily exhaustive and other books could certainly be added to the mix.

There are many versions of Aesop's fables in the public domain. I started with *Aesop's Fables* (Watermill Press), which was published as a children's book, and reworded each fable in a manner more appropriate for a business book. I took details of Aesop's life from two works published more than three hundred years ago: *Life of Aesop* by M. Claude Gaspard Bachet de Mezeriac, published in 1632 (translated by George Fyler Townsend in 1882); and *The Life of Aesop* by Sir Roger L'Estrange, published in 1692. Remarkably, there is a general consensus that modern scholars have not been able to add anything substantive to the information on Aesop's life compiled by these seventeenth-century writers.

Let me explain an important point about the fables and the historical time when Aesop compiled them. The ancient Greeks worshiped many gods. They believed the gods were friendly to mankind and could be angered only by irreverence or impudence. Several of the fables I used mention one or more of the gods from the ancient pantheon. When the Roman culture came in contact with the Greek culture around 500 BC, the Romans began to adopt many of the same gods but called them by different names. Thus, the Greek god Zeus became Jupiter, Hermes became Mercury, Athena became Minerva, and so on. I used the superceding Roman names in those few fables where gods are mentioned. Paul of Tarsus brought Christianity to Greece around AD 51. Theodosius I, the first Christian emperor of Rome, banned all pagan cults in AD 393. In AD 426, Theodosius II ordered all pagan shrines and temples destroyed. Today, 98 percent of Greek citizens are Christians who belong to the Greek Orthodox Church.

Finally, I have integrated tales from some of my experiences in private industry to further illustrate the business lessons. Every story is true, but I have changed the names of some people to protect their privacy.

* * *

I want to thank everyone who offered support, encouragement, and advice as I worked on this book. My parents, John and Arline Noonan, have been role models throughout my life. Clare, my wife of twenty-eight years, has been a constant source of light, strength, and support. My children were true inspirations along every step of this journey: Kristin with her passion and creativity, John with his solid commitment to ethics, and Mark with his pursuit of excellence. I want to thank my aunt, Sister Paschala Noonan, O.P., a gifted writer who provided much timely advice and helped edit the manuscript. Special thanks to Neal O'Connor, who shared his enormous talents by keeping his keen eye on details and by suggesting the book's structural framework. Thanks to others in my family who helped me in various ways: Leone and David Murphy, Barbara and Tom Yost, Bill and Marge Cashman, Cheryl and Tim Cuddihy, Karen Murphy, and Michelle Murphy.

I must say "thank you" to my agent, David Robie, who shared my enthusiasm from the beginning, and who worked hard in getting this book into the right hands.

I offer special thanks to Brian Hampton, my editor at Nelson Business, for his insight, patience, and vision.

I also want to remember my good friend Robert Kane, who relentlessly encouraged me when I started this project, and whose spirit lives on in his wonderful wife, Maureen. Finally, thanks to John Rieppe for planting the seed in his *Business Travel Executive* article, and to David Gaddis for passing the article along to me because he thought I might like it. He was right. I did.

Introduction

Aesop's Life *and* Fables

Aesop (620–560? BC) was born into slavery most likely in Thrace, a large region of the Balkan Peninsula in what's known today as Greece, Bulgaria, and Turkey. Slaves toiled hard as miners, plantation workers, or if they were lucky, household servants. It was possible for a slave to earn freedom (called manumission) through diligent work and loyal service. Aesop, a hunchback with a speech impediment, had two masters during his enslavement. His second owner recognized the exceptional intelligence, wit, and tact of his servant, and as a result, he eventually granted Aesop his freedom. Freed slaves were permitted to engage in civic affairs and to travel wherever they wanted, and Aesop eagerly pursued both opportunities. His reputation grew as a wise and noble man. He traveled extensively to learn as much as he could but also, as he grew older, to impart his wisdom to people in other countries.

Aesop's reputation grew enormously after he arrived in Sardis, the famed capital of Lydia in Asia Minor (now Turkey), which was ruled by King Croesus. Croesus, of "rich as Croesus" fame, was known as a dedicated patron of learning; he allowed Aesop to interact with the great wise men of the day including Solon and Thales, two of the so-called wise men of Greece. Aesop did more than hold his own with these sages, and so impressed Croesus that the king instructed Aesop to make his permanent home in Sardis. During that period, Aesop began to assemble his collection of instructive tales about human behavior. He used the short fables to convey universal truths and lessons about how life should be properly lived. He gave the animals human traits and set them up in various conflicts. The morals were often cautionary. His fables gained wide recognition as people passed them along by word of mouth.

Because of Aesop's keen mind and tactfulness, Croesus enlisted him for various diplomatic missions, sending him to cities like Athens and Corinth. Aesop used his fables to calm tensions, build consensus, and facilitate governance. It was on one of those diplomatic missions that Aesop met his end.

In a particularly generous gesture to his subjects, Croesus sent Aesop to Delphi, home of the Oracle and the most influential religious sanctuary in ancient Greece, to distribute a large amount of gold among the citizenry. But once there, Aesop became disgusted with the greedy and ungrateful nature of the people in the face of such largesse. His attempts, through his fables, to show the people the error of their ways proved futile. Finally, frustrated and disillusioned with the citizens of Delphi, Aesop sent the gold back to Croesus. The people became enraged when they learned what Aesop had done. They ignored his diplomatic status as well as his reputation as a good and wise man, and executed him as a public criminal by hurling him off a cliff.

Not long afterward, Delphi was hit with a series of catastrophes. Many believed the misfortunes were the result of Aesop's unjust murder, and the phrase "beset with the blood of Aesop" became a common adage signifying that bad deeds against another would not go unpunished. The people of Delphi eventually atoned and made amends for their crime against Aesop. Lysippus, a famous Greek sculptor, immortalized the fabulist by erecting a statue of him in Athens.

Aesop's fables continued to be passed along for centuries through oral tradition until around 300 BC when Demetrius Phalereus, an

Athenian politician, compiled about two hundred of the fables in the text *Assemblies of Aesop's Tales*. Three centuries later, another freed Greek slave named Phaedrus translated the collection of stories into Latin for a much broader audience. About AD 230, a Greek poet named Valerius Babrius combined fables from India with their Greek counterparts and published the entire collection in Greek verse. Babrius's simple and charming collection of tales is the most widely read set of fables in world literature today and provides the context for the business tales you are about to read.

Rewards
and
Incentives

No person will make a great business who wants to do it all himself or get all the credit.

—ANDREW CARNEGIE
(U.S. STEEL MANUFACTURER
AND PHILANTHROPIST, 1835–1919)

*Take delight in,
and frequent the company of good people.*

—AESOP

The Hound *and* the Hare

A hare was nibbling away at some plants in a field one day when she noticed a hunter she had never seen before patrolling the area with his hound.

Now I have two new predators to outwit, the animal thought, *and since that hound is a lot younger than I am, he's probably a lot faster too. To off-set the hound's speed, I'll need to know every inch of terrain by heart.*

Seizing the initiative, the hare went out to the fields at supper-time when she knew the hunter was not around. She studied every hiding place, every briar, and the path through every bramble. A few days later, the hound spotted the hare and gave chase. The hare darted through the fields, briars, and underbrush, and she easily escaped. Tired and disappointed, the hound returned to the hunter.

A goatherd passing by saw the whole chase and began to berate the hound. "Some hunter you turned out to be! You ought to be ashamed of yourself, letting a hare so much smaller and older get the better of you."

"You're forgetting one thing," the hound replied. "I was running for my supper, but that hare was running for her life."

{
AESOP'S MORAL:
Initiative is the child of necessity.
}

PERSPECTIVE: Do you think some people, like the hare in the fable, are naturally predisposed to taking the initiative? Do you believe that workers can be taught to take the initiative? Do you suspect that some workers could take the initiative but choose not to because they figure the extra work will go unrecognized? When was the last time you undertook an initiative at work without being asked? Did your extra effort bear fruit? Did others in the organization recognize your initiative? Did it matter to you whether it was recognized or not? Would you take the initiative again?

Organizations are full of intelligent, motivated, and experienced people who lack initiative. I worked with many talented men and women who were ready to do anything the company needed, as long as someone else told them what to do.

Initiative is a fire that burns within an individual. It isn't waiting to be told what to do. It's an innate drive to make a process, system, or product better than it was before. People take initiatives to improve themselves by spending off-hours going to school, learning more about the corporation they work for or the industry they work in. Many people take the initiative not knowing whether their efforts will lead anywhere or benefit anybody. They are driven by the *potential* for new successes. And many of the same people are pleasantly surprised when their initiative reaps benefits much greater than anybody ever expected. In *How to Be a Star at Work*, Robert Kelley describes how one person's initiative resulted in an unprecedented windfall.

For ten years, Kathleen Betts processed Massachusetts' medical bills on behalf of Medicaid patients. But in 1991, the state's $460 million budget shortfall threatened not only her job, but also the jobs of hundreds of state workers and various programs for people with low incomes. Governor William Weld refused to raise taxes to cover the gap.

The thirty-eight-year-old Betts had recently cut back her hours so she could spend more time with her two children, then nine and two years old. But the fact that she worked only three days a week didn't diminish her commitment to her job or impede her initiative. Searching for a way to inject more benefits into the Medicaid system, Betts took home Medicaid manuals and Department of Human Health and Services guidelines. Hour after hour, evening after evening, she scoured the deadly dull documents for a pot of gold.

One day she uncovered a flaw in the way in which state and federal agencies calculated hospital operating costs and income. The upshot? Massachusetts' Medicaid program was receiving much less reimbursement money than it was entitled to. The federal government kicked in an additional $489 million to correct the glitch. Incredibly, one woman's initiative eliminated the state's enormous deficit, saved hundreds of state jobs including her own, and kept fully funded the programs for people with limited financial resources.

Elated, Governor Weld pushed through a bill that provided a $10,000 cash award to Betts and subsequent state employees who make government more productive, stating that "often the best ideas come from the people on the front lines."

"The bonus was just the frosting on the cake," Betts later said. "To me, it was great that the state was recognizing our work and it brought to light some of the positive potential for mothers who want to work. There's so much good that I felt came of it."

"Betts was featured as the ABC News Person of the Week, landed on the front page of the *New York Times,* and was invited to be on David Letterman," Kelley says. "So why was she the nation's darling in the summer of 1991? Why did America fall in love with a state government bureaucrat in, of all places, the public welfare office? Because Kathy Betts had shown initiative."

{ BUSINESS MORAL:
*Personal initiative can mean the difference
between business failure and success.* }

SOURCE

Kelley, Robert Earl. *How to Be a Star at Work: Nine Breakthrough Strategies You Need to Succeed*, 39–41. New York: Times Business, 1998.

The Donkey Eating Thistles

I t was harvesttime, and the master and workers were out in the fields bringing in the crops. The harvest was bountiful, and the master and his family were going to prosper greatly. Lunchtime drew near. To fortify the workers, the servants at the house loaded up a donkey with beverages and good things to eat: breads, cheeses, olives, figs, grapes, and delicious meats.

As the donkey ambled down the path to the workers in the field, he saw a large thistle growing nearby. The animal was hungry and immediately went over to the thistle and began to eat it. As he munched on the prickly plant, the donkey thought, *I bet there are many people who'd love to sample the delicious food I'm carrying on my back. But to my taste, this bitter and thorny thistle is more savory and satisfying than the most lavish banquet.*

{ AESOP'S MORAL:
*One person's meat may
be another person's poison.* }

PERSPECTIVE: What kinds of rewards do you seek at work? Greater responsibilities? A bigger raise? A bigger bonus? Wider recognition among your peers? More time off? What kinds of rewards do you think the person in the office next to you wants? Do you know what kinds of rewards other employees value?

In fact, the rewards that people seek in the workplace vary significantly and depend on the person. Some managers assume that money—in the form of a raise or a bonus—is the most important motivator. But other things, such as recognition, more freedom, more control, time off, or a piece of the action, can be just as important. According to Mary Kay Ash, founder of Mary Kay Cosmetics, "There are two things people want more than sex and money—recognition and praise."

Peggy Noonan, speechwriter for the late President Reagan, understands the power of recognition. Noonan had been working for Reagan for four months and had yet to meet him. One day, Reagan sent back one of her speech drafts with the words *Very Good* written in the margin. This bit of recognition was so exciting to her that she cut out the comment and taped it to her blouse so that everyone could see it for the rest of the day.

In *1001 Ways to Reward Employees*, Bob Nelson stresses the need to match the reward to the person: "Few management concepts are as solidly founded as the idea that positive reinforcement . . . works." He cites Catherine Meek of Meek and Associates for guidelines about what constitutes an effective reward and recognition program:

1. Develop your program so as to reward behavior consistent with the firm's values and business strategy;

2. Let your employees help develop and implement the program;

3. Vary the rewards. Make them informal and formal, cash and non-cash, individual and team;

4. Publicize the program and the employees who receive the rewards;

5. Change the program frequently; otherwise it will lose its vitality and power to motivate.

Let me offer a personal example of what can happen if you don't match the reward to the employee. Several years ago, I met with Edgar, a top scientist in our firm, to conduct his annual performance review. He was a brilliant man and a hard worker who had received stellar marks for performance that year. I asked him how the company could best reward him for his hard work over the past twelve months.

First, he told me what he didn't want. "Believe it or not," Edgar said, "I don't want a big raise. I'm well paid as it is, and if you give me a big raise, you'll start pricing me out of the market. People will be more reluctant to use me on their projects because my hourly rate will become an even greater burden. I could price myself right out of a job."

He then went on to explain what he really wanted: "There is a one-week conference later next year that I would like the company to let me attend. It will help me expand my technical capabilities, make me even more valuable to the firm, and satisfy my need for an intellectual challenge. Instead of money, give me time off to attend the conference."

I took his request to the regional manager. Incredibly, the manager said, "We can't give Edgar seven days off for the conference. But we can give him a nice raise." The manager's rationale was straightforward: the conference budget was based on four employees attending two-day seminars. Edgar's request would use up seven of the eight allotted days. The manager subsequently gave him a large raise but denied him permission to attend the conference. The sad fact was that the cost to the company of letting him attend the conference was a lot less than the raise we gave him. As you might expect, a frustrated Edgar left the firm the following year.

People's motivations will change over time with monetary rewards potentially becoming less of a motivator as they move up the ladder. According to Sumner Redstone, CEO of Viacom, "Most people who succeed in significant areas do not succeed because of a desire for money."

{
BUSINESS MORAL:
Pay raises and bonuses may fail to motivate employees seeking recognition, praise, or time off.
}

SOURCES

Nelson, Bob. *1001 Ways to Reward Employees,* xvii, 4. New York: Workman Publishers, 1994.

Noonan, Peggy. *What I Saw at the Revolution*, 64. New York: Random House, 1990.

Redstone, Sumner. "What I've Learned." *Esquire,* January 2003, 64.

The Donkey Carrying Salt

A merchant decided to take a load of salt to market, so he placed sacks of salt on his donkey and set off for town. The road was close to a slippery ledge. As they passed the ledge, the donkey stumbled and fell into the stream below. The water melted the salt, relieving the beast of his burden. The unhappy merchant returned home and loaded the donkey a second time.

I'm sick of carrying things, especially salt, the donkey thought to himself. *If I keep falling into the water, I can keep getting rid of these loads.*

The second time the donkey approached the slope, he intentionally lost his footing and fell in. By then, the merchant had caught on to the donkey's trick. On the next journey, he loaded the animal with sponges. When the donkey fell into the stream, he found himself struggling under a load that had more than doubled in weight.

{
A ESOP'S MORAL:
Counter old tricks with new ones.
}

PERSPECTIVE: If only the donkey had realized the importance of his work. Salt had religious significance in ancient times. The Hebrews rubbed salt on newborn babies to ensure good health. At one time, salt was so scarce that it was used as money. Caesar's soldiers received part of their pay in salt. Had it been possible, the merchant might have stopped the animal's antics by appealing to the natural need to be part of something bigger and more meaningful. The donkey might have hauled the load proudly, knowing the salt was going to be used to protect infants or pay soldiers' wages to keep the peace.

What do you do for a living? Do you consider your work just a job? Does it give you a sense of mission? Or are you merely biding your time until something better comes along?

I've been fortunate in this regard. After I graduated from college, I got a job working to improve the environment as a water resources engineer, but I always considered it more than a job—it was a calling. My company hired a gang of other like-minded grads at the same time. Brent, Dan, Davey, Joe, John, Ken, and I believed we weren't just putting in forty hours and receiving paychecks; we were making the environment safer and healthier, acting as good stewards to preserve the natural world and, in some small way, restoring Eden. That belief never left us. Thirty years later, every one of us is still involved in, and committed to, improving the environment. Our work continues to have a higher purpose.

Former U.S. Secretary of Labor Robert Reich once said,

> Work has always been more than just an economic transaction. It helps define who we are. It confirms our usefulness. What we do on the job . . . gives meaning and dignity to our lives. Dignity at work is not simply a matter of status and power. Dignity depends in large part, I think, on whether one feels valued. And the sense of being valued at work comes both from appreciation shown by others and from one's own pride in doing a job well, no matter how humble. In this respect, work is a moral act as well as an economic one.

Every worker can have the power of higher purpose, no matter where she is on the organizational ladder. Consider the case of Shirley, a housekeeper in a 250-bed community hospital. She is just one of 200,000 workers employed by ServiceMaster, a conglomerate serving more than 6 million customers in 31 countries. Companies within the ServiceMaster family include TruGreen, ChemLawn, Terminix, and Merry Maids. C. William Pollard is the former CEO and chairman of ServiceMaster. In *The Soul of the Firm*, he says that Shirley was merely looking for a job at first. Her attitude changed after she was hired. Her housekeeping job became her cause. "If we don't clean with a quality effort," Shirley explained, "we can't keep the doctors and nurses in business; we can't accommodate patients. This place would be *closed* if we didn't have housekeeping."

Shirley's mission is greater: she is part of a team that helps sick people get better. Pollard believes that managers get the best results when they harness the power of purpose: "People want to work for a cause, not just for a living."

{ **BUSINESS MORAL:**
Inspire workers by helping them understand that their work has a higher purpose. }

SOURCES

Pollard, C. William. *The Soul of the Firm,* 45–47. New York: HarperBusiness; Grand Rapids, MI: Zondervan Publishing House, 1996.

Reich, Robert. "The Moral Basis of Our Labor." *Boston Globe,* September 2, 1996, A19.

Jupiter *and* the Bee

B ack in the days when gods ruled the earth, an industrious bee was laboring diligently in the apiary of his master. This bee was just one of many going about the business of making honeycombs.

Thrilled with the sweetness of his own honey, the bee thought to himself: *This honey is fit for a god. I think I'll fly to the heavens and present it to Jupiter as a gift.*

The god was delighted with the present and promised the bee anything he wanted in return.

"Great Jupiter, master of all, give your humble servant a sting so powerful that when anyone approaches my hive to take my honey, I may kill him instantly," the bee said.

Jupiter was dismayed at the request because one of the visitors to the hive would certainly be the beekeeper, who was responsible for all of the hives. Angry, Jupiter scolded the bee: "You bloodthirsty creature. I'll grant your wish but not exactly how you'd hoped. You shall have the sting. When anyone approaches your hive and you attack, the wound shall be fatal—but *to you*. You shall lose your life along with your sting."

{
A ESOP'S MORAL:
*Plotting against your neighbor
will bring misfortune upon you.*
}

14

PERSPECTIVE: Giving bonuses is one way that companies seek to reward good work by employees. But one of the more contentious tasks faced by management is how to apportion bonuses fairly among a group of worthy individuals.

Why do companies give bonuses and other financial rewards in the first place? What's their purpose? Why do you think most companies don't publicize what individuals receive for bonuses? If an employee had a spectacular year, but the business unit in which he worked did not, should he receive a bonus? Conversely, if a business unit greatly exceeded all financial expectations in a given year, but several individuals within that unit performed poorly, should those people receive bonuses?

Ideally, the purpose of rewards should be to acknowledge outstanding individual contributions to a company's overall success. The ways to divide up the bonus pie, however, tend to be as numerous as the people eligible for those bonuses. Many people tend to believe that they contributed more to the firm's bottom line than their colleagues and, consequently, should receive a bigger bonus. Companies also have to be careful to reward performance that they want repeated in the future. Some companies unintentionally give bonuses for behavior that they *don't* want repeated. Alfred P. Sloan Jr. explained what was wrong with General Motors in *My Years with General Motors*.

GM reorganized into divisions to decentralize operations and give managers more autonomy. The problem was that key executives had little incentive to think in terms of the welfare of the whole firm. Under the existing incentive system, each division was a profit center, and executive bonuses were tied strictly to how well each division performed. Sloan described the problem: "This system exaggerated the self-interest of each division at the expense of the interests of the corporation itself. It was even possible for a division manager to act contrary to the interests of the corporation."

Sloan realized that managers were looking out for their own divisions and paying little attention to the bigger picture of how GM was doing as a firm. He worked to revamp the bonus plan to reflect the need for each executive to be aware of the corporation's overall well-being by stressing the importance of putting corporate profits ahead of divisional profits.

GM ran into another problem related to dishing out bonuses: employees expected them every year as part of their rightful compensation. Sloan was forced to make it clear that bonuses depended on whether the company made a profit. He told employees that they should expect bonuses to vary from year to year, depending on how the company fared. In a bold but enlightened move at the time, he also expanded the number of people who qualified for a bonus by including employees who contributed to the company's success in a variety of ways, such as their "inventions, ability, industry, loyalty or exceptional service."

{
BUSINESS MORAL:
*Putting self-interest ahead of the greater
corporate good eventually will lead to failure.*
}

SOURCE

Sloan, Alfred P. *My Years with General Motors,* 409. New York: Doubleday/Currency, 1963.

Management
and
Leadership
(Communicating Effectively)

God can dream a bigger dream for us than we could ever dream for ourselves. The key to realizing a dream is to focus not on success but significance—and then even the small steps . . . along your path will take on greater meaning.

—OPRAH WINFREY
(CHAIRMAN, HARPO ENTERTAINMENT GROUP, 1954–)

Rise early to your business, learn good things, and oblige good people. These are three things you shall never repent of.

—AESOP

The Monkey *and* the Dolphin

I n olden days, sailors took pets aboard ships to amuse the crew while they were at sea. On one particular voyage, a sailor brought aboard a monkey as a companion. A violent storm battered the ship just as it neared Attica, a peninsula that juts into the Aegean Sea. The waves eventually dashed the boat to pieces, throwing everyone into the water, including the monkey. A dolphin spotted the monkey struggling in the angry seas and, believing him to be a human, offered to ride the animal to shore on his back.

The dolphin swam easily in the foaming water, and soon the pair drew closer to land just opposite Piraeus, the harbor to the city of Athens.

"Are you an Athenian?" the dolphin asked.

"Yes, I am," lied the monkey. "I belong to one of the most prominent families in all of Athens."

"Then you must know Piraeus," the dolphin said proudly, referring to the beautiful harbor where he made his home.

Thinking Piraeus must be a distinguished official, the monkey replied, "Yes, I do. He's one of my dearest friends."

When the dolphin heard the obvious lie, he dived to the bottom of the sea, leaving the monkey to drown.

{
AESOP'S MORAL:
*Those who pretend to be something they
are not will eventually be found out.*
}

PERSPECTIVE: What qualities do you think make a leader exceptional? Do you think charisma is essential? Intelligence? A keen business sense? The ability to engage people at various organizational levels? Does a great leader have to be a great communicator or an inspiring orator? All of these talents and qualities are excellent ones, and most leaders have them in different combinations. But if you are like most people, you believe that one quality outranks them all. In survey after survey and poll after poll, workers insist that *integrity* is the hallmark of every great leader.

Employees want to know, above all, that they can trust their leaders. That bond of trust is especially important during turbulent times, when the waters of instability and uncertainty are swirling about. People can bear up under bad news, particularly if they know their leaders are communicating the facts honestly and are working hard to get a bad situation under control. I know. Our company faced a potentially disastrous situation back in the 1980s. Let me explain.

The environmental consulting industry was flat. Companies were consolidating, competition was intensifying, and profit margins were shrinking. We decided to expand our business into real estate where we expected profit margins to be much higher. The plan was to buy old mill buildings around New England, use our in-house architects to refurbish them as condominiums, and sell them at a nice profit. The plan was well conceived, but ill timed: the condo market in the Northeast collapsed just as we were putting up the "For Sale" signs.

The hit to the company's bottom line was devastating. Bonuses dried up for several years, all new business ventures ceased, and cost cutting became an obsession. To his credit, though, our CEO kept all the employees informed of how bad the losses were and what the company was doing to solve the problem. He gave continuous updates on the company's progress, presented a timetable for extricating the firm from its financial problems, and reassured every employee that the company could and would withstand the financial crisis. We did. Moreover, the CEO emerged as a man of integrity who gave us honest answers when we most needed them.

But what if a leader doesn't have all of the answers? What if the situation isn't under control? What if the situation is so unpredictable that no one can provide meaningful answers in the short term? Is there anything a leader can do to allay fears or calm concerns?

Rudolph Giuliani found himself in a swirling sea of uncertainty in the wake of the terrorist attacks on New York City on September 11. People were anxious and frightened. They demanded definitive answers about when conditions would return to normal. But the situation was so unprecedented, so catastrophic, that nobody, including Giuliani, could give definitive answers. Giuliani explains what it was like and how he handled the situation in his book *Leadership*.

One of the first questions people asked, Giuliani says, was when they could start flying again. Initially, the FAA said that normal air traffic would resume by noon *the next day*! In fact, by that Friday, only a few general aviation flights had actually taken off. "Often, someone who is being pressed for deadlines will sputter something out," Giuliani states. "I do my best to anticipate those questions; but when you don't know the answer, you've got to be honest enough to say so." He notes that transportation routes were a mess after the attacks.

The Holland Tunnel was closed. To relieve congestion, the city allowed only automobiles with two or more passengers to use the bridges. Even then, commuting was going to be a lot worse than usual, especially because truckloads of debris had to be removed from downtown Manhattan, so access was restricted. Giuliani reports, "Sure, I'd like to have set everyone's mind at ease by announcing 'everything is fine, come on back through the Holland Tunnel.' But the comfort people would have felt from hearing that would have been undone as soon as they hit the traffic jams." He believed it was better to say that he didn't know when the city's traffic would return to normal rather than fake it and have people lose confidence in his ability to lead.

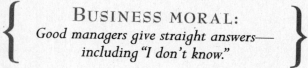

{ BUSINESS MORAL:
*Good managers give straight answers—
including "I don't know."* }

SOURCE
Giuliani, Rudolph W. *Leadership,* 165–66. New York: Hyperion, 2002.

The Rooster *and* the Jewel

O ne summer's day, a rooster scoured the barnyard looking for food. As he scratched at the straw on the ground, he uncovered a jewel. The rooster suspected the jewel might be valuable because of the way it glittered in the sun.

This object is probably worth a lot, the rooster thought to himself, *but I'd trade a bushel of these shiny things for a single kernel of corn.*

{
AESOP'S MORAL:
Preciousness is in the eye of the beholder.
}

PERSPECTIVE: If the rooster had seen the big picture, he would have realized that the jewel could have been sold for a great deal of money, and the money used to buy large stores of grain. But he didn't appreciate the jewel's value. Instead, he focused on his immediate need to forage for scraps. Sometimes employees unexpectedly uncover "jewels" within a company but don't appreciate the value of what they find, like the manager whom Sam Walton describes in his autobiography, *Sam Walton: Made in America.*

Walton and Tom Coughlin, another company executive, made it a habit to routinely visit Wal-Mart stores. Like McDonald's Ray Kroc, Walton strongly believed that store visits could provide new ideas on how to improve business. One day, Walton and Coughlin decided to visit a store in Crowley, Louisiana, managed by Dan McAllister.

As Walton and Coughlin walked around the store, they noticed Dan standing at the front of the building greeting customers. Dan impressed Walton with his ability to make each customer feel warm and welcome. While the greetings made people feel good, the real reason the manager had stationed himself so conspicuously was to prevent people from walking out the entrance with merchandise— shoplifters had beset the store. Tom Coughlin explains, "Dan McAllister . . . knew how to take care of his inventory. He didn't want to intimidate the honest customers by posting a guard at the door, but he wanted to leave a clear message that if you came in and stole, someone was there who would see it."

Walton thought having a greeter at the front of the store, sending a warm, friendly message to customers, was a gem of an idea, and he decided to post a greeter at every store in the country. Walton's insistence on posting greeters won out against the strong objections of other senior Wal-Mart executives. "I guess his vindication had to be the day in 1989 when he walked into a Kmart in Illinois and found that they had installed people greeters at their front doors," Coughlin says.

The marketplace is filled with employees' great ideas; McDonald's Big Mac sandwich, 3M's Post-it Notes, Sony's Walkman, and Dunkin' Donuts' Munchkins are other examples of what can happen when companies unlock the creativity of their workers.

Does your company encourage input from employees on ways to improve business? What means of communication can a worker use to float a gem of an idea up to your senior management? Suggestion boxes are a good start, but even more powerful means exist in this electronic age. Many companies have internal e-mail addresses through which workers can offer suggestions directly to management.

Whatever method you use, make sure that you respond to every person who offers a suggestion, even if you don't intend to use it. Let workers know that you value their input on any facet of the business they think can be improved. And if any idea turns out to be a gem, publicly acknowledge the person who came up with it to encourage other employees to come forward. Continuous improvement begins on the front line.

{
BUSINESS MORAL:
Encourage every employee to uncover gems of ideas hidden in the organization.
}

SOURCE
Walton, Sam. *Sam Walton: Made in America,* 229–30. New York: Doubleday, 1992.

The Rooster *and* the Fox

A fox walking near a farmyard one morning heard a rooster crowing. Exploring further, the fox found the rooster perched in a tree out of reach.

"Friend Rooster," the fox politely said, "it's nice to see you on such a pleasant day. Please come down from your perch so that we might chat."

The rooster was naturally suspicious and replied, "I dare not because there are many animals that would like to have me for breakfast."

"You mean you haven't heard the news?" the fox said excitedly. "All the animals have agreed to live together in peace. Nobody will hurt you now."

The rooster wanted to believe the fox but was skeptical that such a startling development could take place without his knowledge. He craned his neck looking out at the horizon.

The fox noticed the rooster looking around and asked, "What's so interesting that you're ignoring me?"

"It seems we are about to have some company," replied the rooster. "A pack of hounds is coming this way."

"Please excuse me," the fox said anxiously, "but I need to tend to something in my den."

The rooster replied, "Please don't go! I was just about to come down to talk to you and the dogs about this remarkable peace plan."

"It just might be possible," the fox said as she scampered away, "that the hounds haven't yet heard of the plan."

{ AESOP'S MORAL:
*The worst liars often get
tangled in their own lies.* }

PERSPECTIVE: Managers are constantly inundated with information, some of it accurate, some of it not. The problem becomes one of deciding what to believe. How do you get your information at work? From whom do you get it? Do you trust your sources? Have they ever been wrong? What do you do when somebody gives you information that you find hard to believe or that strikes you as not entirely accurate? Colin Powell faced this dilemma when he visited the Middle East at a very critical time. Oren Harari describes what went through Powell's mind in *The Leadership Secrets of Colin Powell.*

Back in 1978, the army ordered Powell to fly to Tehran, the capital of Iran, to assess the stability of the Shah's regime. American agents were picking up rumors that Muslim fundamentalists, incited by the Ayatollah Khomeini, planned to oust the Shah. The rumors seemed far-fetched: How could an elderly man living in exile in Paris orchestrate a government overthrow thousands of miles away?

The Shah greeted Powell warmly and made him the guest of honor at several large banquets. Powell attended military parades and air shows where the armed forces proudly displayed state-of-the-art weaponry and aircraft. The Shah assured Powell that the regime was in control and that the general population supported him. If anyone tried to overthrow him, he told Powell, his crack troops, called the "Immortals," would fight to the death for him.

Powell listened to the Shah and the Iranian military leaders but didn't quite believe them. A voice inside told him something wasn't quite right. Powell personally witnessed numerous street skirmishes between police and the fundamentalist groups. Obviously, the Shah wasn't in complete control. Worse, a U.S. Air Force captain stationed in Tehran told Powell that the Iranian troops were far from battle ready.

Troubled by the conflicting accounts he heard, Powell left Iran unsure what to believe. Three months later, he learned his instincts were right when fundamentalists took over the country, toppled the Peacock Throne, and sent the Shah into exile. Powell explained, "All our investment came to naught. When the Shah fell, our Iran policy fell with him. All the billions we had spent there only exacerbated conditions."

Listen to your inner voice when it comes to business as well. "The effective leader looks hard at the evidence that's being presented by the people under his or her command, and runs a gut check," says Harari. Effective leaders have to ask themselves: *Do I believe what I'm hearing?*

> { **BUSINESS MORAL:**
> *Trust your instincts and don't believe everything you hear.* }

SOURCE

Harari, Oren. *The Leadership Secrets of Colin Powell,* 83–85. New York: McGraw-Hill, 2002.

The Goatherd *and* the Goats

O ne wintry day when the wind was howling fiercely and snow was falling in blankets, a man and his son drove their goats into a nearby cave for protection. Surprisingly, they found the cave already occupied by a herd of wild goats. The goatherd was a greedy man and wanted to keep all of the goats. So he put his herd in the hands of his son and sent them outside to withstand the storm while he tended to the wild goats inside.

"B-b-but, Father," the son stammered. "I've never tended a herd by myself—I'm not sure what I'm supposed to do."

"You're a bright boy and will figure it out, my son. Don't you see the opportunity? If we keep the wild goats, we'll more than double the size of our herd and, as a result, the money in our pockets."

The goatherd spent the night in the cave, making sure the wild goats didn't escape. The next morning, when the weather cleared, the goatherd looked outside only to see that his own flock had frozen to death. His son was apologetic.

"Father, I didn't know what to do to save them," he lamented.

As the goatherd mourned his dead herd, the wild goats ran to the cave entrance, saw their chance to escape, and fled into the forest. The goatherd and his son returned to town with nothing.

{ AESOP'S MORAL:
*Blame only yourself when you delegate
a task to the unprepared.* }

PERSPECTIVE: The best leaders surround themselves with talented people and then delegate as much as possible to them. One thing a manager must do to delegate effectively is to make sure a worker is ready for the assignment. The more important the assignment, the greater the need for seamless delegation because bad delegation can result in a lot of frozen goat meat. Do you remember Howard Johnson's? Do you remember what happened when Howard Johnson, who built an empire from scratch, handed over the business to his son? In case you don't, take a seat at the lunch counter, and read on.

Howard D. Johnson, with only an eighth-grade education, began his business in 1925. He bought a newsstand and a medicine store next to a train station in Quincy, Massachusetts, and added a soda fountain. He took one of his mother's recipes and made different kinds of ice cream that were rich in butterfat. People loved all "28 Flavors."

Using ice cream as a springboard, he opened more roadside restaurants. The father was a visionary entrepreneur who capitalized on the interstate highways built by the Eisenhower administration after the Second World War. Soon, hundreds of restaurants blossomed along toll roads, turnpikes, and highways in the eastern United States. He also established motor lodges adjoining the restaurants to further capitalize on America's love affair with the automobile. The synergy was stunning and fueled tremendous growth.

But as the company was hitting its stride and expanding quickly, the father—suddenly and inexplicably—resigned and put his son in charge. When he left in 1960, Howard Johnson delegated to his son, Howard B. Johnson, an American business icon with more than seven hundred easily-recognizable restaurants with their bright orange roofs and cupolas capped by Simple Simon and the Pie Man weather vanes. The sheer momentum created by the father's vision kept the company growing for several years after his departure. In fact, in 1965, Ho Jo's sales were more than those of Burger King, McDonald's, and Kentucky Fried Chicken combined. But his son was not up to the task of sustaining such a large company over the long haul, particularly when consumer trends were changing so rapidly in the late 1960s and early 1970s.

Howard Johnson's son did the only thing he knew how to do: in effect, he became an accountant, constantly looking for ways to cut costs and avoid *any* long-term debt. The company did little marketing, pinched pennies on menus and staffing, and failed to upgrade its buildings. *Forbes* quotes one of Ho Jo's competitors: "Every time I saw Howard Johnson [the son] he was always telling me how he was going to cut costs further. I don't think he spent enough time at his restaurants. If he'd eaten in his own restaurants more instead of lunching at '21' [a posh New York restaurant], he might have learned something."

Because he was in over his head, the son couldn't see the enormous opportunities at his feet if he changed the company's business plan. Ho Jo's could have concentrated on being a coffee shop, but Denny's woke up to the opportunity first. The company could have concentrated on ice cream, but Baskin-Robbins and Häagen-Dazs took it head-on and licked it. Howard Johnson's could have concentrated on fast food, but McDonald's, Burger King, and KFC ate its lunch, principally because the relative newcomers specialized in one type of menu and located restaurants in towns off exit ramps instead of on the highway. Howard Johnson's could have concentrated on frozen foods, but didn't want to invest the required $10 million, thereby letting Stouffer's freeze it out. The company could have focused on motels, but Holiday Inn and Marriott left it no room to grow profitably.

Stuck in a land of missed opportunities and rising prices, Ho Jo's was forced to start closing restaurants and motels during the 1970s. A British conglomerate, the Imperial Group, bought Ho Jo's for

$630 million in December 1979 in a well-intentioned attempt to turn it around. But the sad reality was that Ho Jo's time had come and gone. Worse, the foreign buyers had no idea how badly Ho Jo's reputation and facilities had declined. Realizing the acquisition was a big mistake, Imperial sold the company six years later for $300 million—less than half the original purchase price.

When he delegated the leadership to his son and walked away, Howard Johnson set in motion the forces that would lead to the sad decline of an American institution. Effective delegation requires managers to remain involved. You can increase the chances that a delegated task will be done to your satisfaction if you follow these steps, says Robert Nelson in *Delegation: The Power of Letting Go*:

- Specify exactly what the task entails and how it fits into the bigger picture.

- Specify the performance parameters the person must meet, including how much money is budgeted, the date the work must be completed by, and the level of accuracy needed (i.e., whether the answer can be an estimate or must be calculated to three significant figures).

- Empower the person with the authority to access other people who might be needed to complete the task.

- Free up the resources (e.g., marketing, human resources, supplies, audiovisuals, graphics support, etc.) needed elsewhere in the firm to support the person.

- Obtain the personal commitment of the person taking over the task.

- Periodically monitor and evaluate how the person is performing.

This last point is critical, especially if the person assuming the task is relatively inexperienced. Periodic monitoring also ensures that you get bad news in a timely manner. It's simple prudence to anticipate problems the subordinate might encounter, as well as develop contingency plans in case something goes wrong.

If the goatherd and Howard Johnson had only checked from time to time on how their sons were faring, the final outcomes would likely have been much different.

{
BUSINESS MORAL:
When you delegate, it's your responsibility to make sure that person successfully completes the assignment.
}

SOURCES

Merwin, John. "The Sad Case of the Dwindling Orange Roofs." *Forbes,* December 30, 1985, 79.

Nelson, Robert B. *Delegation: The Power of Letting Go,* 73–76, 81–82, 85–86, 92–97. Glenview, IL: Scott Foresman and Company, 1988.

The Mice in Council

A large group of mice lived in a barn for many years. Life was wonderful, except for the sneaky cat that prowled around. Hardly a day went by without a poor mouse being chased or even eaten by the cat. Finally, the head mouse called a meeting.

"Ladies and gentlemen, youngsters and baby mice," he stated. "The time is now to resolve our problems with the cat. Does anyone have any solutions?"

The mice were abuzz with ideas and suggestions, but none seemed to solve the problem.

Then a young mouse got up, took the floor, and said boldly, "Let's hang a bell around the cat's neck. That way, whenever the cat is near, we'll hear the ringing and safely hide." The crowd applauded loudly as the mouse took his seat.

Once the applause died down, an elderly mouse rose to his feet and said, "Our young friend's plan is simple yet ingenious. Once the bell is on the cat, we'll all live safely. But I have one brief question to put to you all: Which one of you will volunteer to bell the cat?"

{ AESOP'S MORAL:
*It is much easier to propose
than to execute.* }

PERSPECTIVE: How many meetings did you attend this week? How many of them did you think were productive? A meeting can be a curse or a blessing, wasteful or useful; it all depends on how well the meeting is run. How many times have you been trapped in a conference room, the clock seemingly moving backward, your eyes glazing over as the conversation wanders pointlessly into unrelated topics? How many times have you thought to yourself: *We could have taken care of business in thirty minutes instead of wasting two hours of everybody's time*? How often have you wanted to let out a liquid scream or make a break for the elevator as a meeting balkanized into a bunch of meaningless sidebar conversations? "Meetings are indispensable when you don't want to do anything," John Kenneth Galbraith once said.

Now here's the bad news: as frustrating as meetings can be, they're absolutely essential to business. Meetings help us brainstorm ideas, solve problems, develop action plans, and create new strategies. Big issues may require multiple meetings. The mice will obviously need a few more productive sessions to solve their cat problem.

Given that meetings are a necessary evil, the question then becomes how to make them as efficient as possible. I have several suggestions based on my experience: have no more than ten people attend the meeting; any more than that becomes unwieldy and requires a lot more crowd control. Be on time. If you are late, you send a clear but incorrect message that your time is more valuable than that of others in the room. People are more likely to be punctual if you set an odd start time, say 2:15 p.m. Confirm how long you expect the meeting to run. Don't meet longer than one hour if possible; after that, people's interest naturally starts to wane. Tolerate no interruptions. Keep the door closed, and tell participants to turn off their cell phones. Finally, when somebody unintentionally impedes the meeting's progress, nicely stop the person, whether she's way off track ("Interesting idea, Paula. Perhaps we could come back to that.") or he's belaboring a point ("Great suggestion, Paul. Let me stop you there. What do the rest of you think of Paul's idea?").

Let's move from an *efficient* meeting to an *effective* meeting. It takes hard work and a good road map to run an effective meeting. Done correctly, though, a meeting can become something to look forward to instead of something to duck. Want to make your meetings more effective? Here are eight steps from *First Among Equals* by Patrick McKenna and David Maister[1]:

1. *Set a singular focus.* The group should devote most of its time to one important issue, recognizing that some time may be spent on housekeeping business.

2. *Brainstorm ideas.* Permit everyone to speak and say anything that comes to mind. There should be no discussion or value judgments, either positive or negative.

3. *Ensure ideas are actionable.* The group should discuss how the ideas mesh with the overall goal. Can the group identify a tangible outcome?

4. *Get voluntary commitments.* Engaging in more discussion may be informative but unproductive. Better to draw out people who are willing to provide a small amount of constructive action in the hopes of building a bit of momentum.

5. *Keep commitments small.* Break the action list into small, doable items. Don't overwhelm the volunteers willing to contribute.

---

1. Adapted with the permission of The Free Press, a Division of Simon & Schuster Adult Publishing Group, from FIRST AMONG EQUALS: How to manage a group of pofessionals by Patrick J. McKenna and David H. Maister. Copyright © 2002 by Partick J. McKenna and David H. Maister. All right reserved.

6. *Establish contracts for action*. Get consensus about who's doing what and when. Identify ways that preliminary results will be shared.

7. *Follow up between meetings*. Let people know that their contributions are important to you. Track their progress. Try to avoid having someone neglect his contribution until the eleventh hour.

8. *Celebrate success*. Spread the good news about accomplishments around the firm. People like to be on winning teams. Sharing success will increase the likelihood that people will show up early for your next meeting.

> { **BUSINESS MORAL:**
> *Run your meetings well to greatly increase the chances of accomplishing your goals.* }

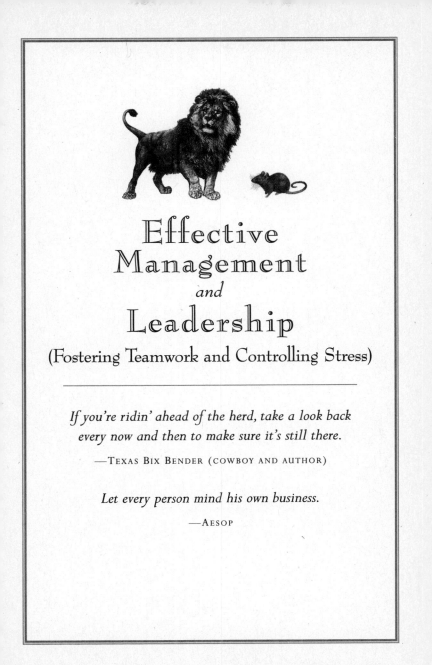

Effective
Management
and
Leadership
(Fostering Teamwork and Controlling Stress)

---

*If you're ridin' ahead of the herd, take a look back
every now and then to make sure it's still there.*

—Texas Bix Bender (cowboy and author)

Let every person mind his own business.

—Aesop

The Bundle of Sticks

A farmer had many sons who quarreled constantly. He tried to mediate the many disputes, offering his wise counsel to get them to stop bickering—to no avail. One day, the irritated farmer reached the end of his patience. He summoned his sons to the barn where a bundle of sticks lay on the ground.

"I want each one of you to step up and try breaking this bundle in two," he said.

Each son tried but couldn't do it. The farmer then untied the bundle and handed each son a stick that he easily broke in two.

The wise farmer then said, "Learn from this example. As long as you remain united, there's no enemy that can break you. But if you separate from one another, you can be ruined."

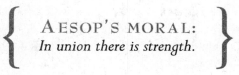

{ AESOP'S MORAL:
In union there is strength. }

PERSPECTIVE: "Recognize the power of the team; no one succeeds alone," says Carly Fiorina, CEO of Hewlett-Packard. Most companies value teamwork and a shared commitment to success. Have you or someone you know ever been hospitalized? A hospital is a perfect example of seamless teamwork in action. Your doctor may be in charge of treatment, but she relies on a team of professionals such as the X-ray technician, blood specialist, laboratory worker, night nurse, and anesthesiologist to figure out what's wrong with you and then to help you get better. Each specialist contributes his talents with few overlapping responsibilities.

Although the hospital model presents one team configuration, there is a different model that works even more effectively when the organization or the type of work is less complex. Let's call it the zoo model. Harvey Seifter describes how it works in *Leadership Ensemble*.

The San Diego Zoo is one of the biggest and most popular zoos in the United States. Each year, more than 5 million people marvel at the 850 species of animals and 6,500 varieties of plants. How much money do you think it takes to run such a large institution? Would you believe that the zoo's annual budget was more than $100 million in 2003? More impressively, the zoo receives almost no public funding; it relies on admission fees and membership dues for its income. Visitors and patrons expect the park to be clean, the animals to be well cared for, and the overall experience to be thoroughly engaging. Teamwork is essential to meet such high expectations.

When Douglas Meyers took over as the zoo's executive director, there were more than fifty separate departments involved in running the facility—an administrative nightmare. Each department had a specific responsibility, such as maintenance, horticulture, or animal keeping. Under Doug's direction, the zoo began integrating self-managed teams by training team members to do *all* of the needed tasks. He assembled teams from different departments that were capable of doing *any* job in the area of the zoo assigned to them.

Seifter explains: "Each team is responsible for every aspect of the area, from maintenance to animal and plant care and includes specialized staff including custodial staff, animal keepers, horti-culturists, and even construction managers. These teams, which usually aren't larger than twelve to fifteen people, have their own operating budgets and are totally responsible for how their budgets are spent."

The integrated team approach provides flexibility and shared responsibility. By broadly defining the job, zoo employees learn more and make themselves more valuable to the organization and more helpful to one another.

{ BUSINESS MORAL:
It's good business to promote teamwork. }

SOURCE

Seifter, Harvey. *Leadership Ensemble: Lessons in Collaborative Management from the World's Only Conductorless Orchestra,* 123–25. New York: Times Books, 2001.

The Fox *and* the Grapes

A hungry fox strolled into a vineyard and saw a lush bunch of ripe grapes hanging from a vine. He jumped as high as he could, but the grapes were out of his reach. Even with a running start, he couldn't grab the juicy payoff. Eventually, the frustrated fox slinked away, muttering, "I'm sure the grapes were sour anyway."

{ AESOP'S MORAL:
*People learn to despise
what they cannot get.* }

PERSPECTIVE: The fox's goal was in view but out of reach. He quickly became frustrated and demoralized. Companies set goals each year that require employees to stretch and grow. But if the goals are unrealistic, then employees become frustrated and unmotivated.

For many years, my company had a very simple rule for setting sales goals for the following year: "Add 15 percent to whatever you did last year." No matter what we accomplished in a given year, we knew that senior management would increase the goal by 15 percent the next year, regardless of what the economy was doing. In some years, the economy was flat, and the goals were too high. We eventually improved the way we set goals each year by soliciting input from every person in marketing and sales, estimating the expected value of new business prospects, and factoring in projected economic conditions. Now, goals are grounded in reality, fair, and in most cases, attainable with effort.

"Set attainable goals," advises Duke University's basketball coach, Mike Krzyzewski, in *Leading with the Heart*. Coach K says he never makes a goal for the team that requires a certain number of wins because it would limit the team's potential.

"Suppose, for instance, that I say our goal for the coming year is to win twenty games and go to the NCAA tournament. If the team wins twenty games and makes it to the tournament, is that the end of it?" Coach K prefers to set goals that are attainable. For example, he told his 1991 team that they could be the best defensive team the school ever had.

"Notice I didn't specifically mention winning or losing ball games," explains Coach K. "However, if a team works at becoming the best defensive team possible, they will put themselves in a position to win every ball game. And I believe, over the course of the year, they'll win more games than if a number, say twenty, was set for the goal."

In fact, Duke's 1991 team did become the best defensive team in the university's history. In addition, they made the NCAA tournament with a 24–2 record and won the national championship.

{
BUSINESS MORAL:
Goals set too high are
invitations for making excuses.
}

SOURCE

Krzyzewski, Mike. *Leading with the Heart: Coach K's Successful Strategies for Basketball, Business and Life,* 60, 64. New York: Warner Books, 2000.

The Horse *and* the Laden Donkey

A man owned a horse and a donkey. He typically loaded the donkey so heavily that the poor creature could barely stand. The horse usually had only a small load and was quite free to trot about.

Both animals were heading down the road one day behind their master when the donkey pleaded, "Friend Horse, the weight of this load is too much. I don't think I can carry it much longer. Can you take at least some of the load off so that I can regain my strength?"

The horse, content with his own workload, ignored the donkey's request and continued on his way.

After staggering a bit farther, the donkey collapsed to the ground, dead. The master took the load off the dead animal and put it on the horse's back. Then he placed the donkey's carcass atop the load.

"It serves me right for not helping out earlier," the horse groaned. "Now I have to carry the donkey's load plus the weight of my dead companion."

{
AESOP'S MORAL:
An uncooperative attitude carries with it its own penalties.
}

PERSPECTIVE: Simone Weil, the French social philosopher, once said, "Nothing in the world can make up for the lack of joy in one's work." What aspects of your job make you happy? In what ways does

46

your job enhance your life? How has your job changed in the past two years? How much has your workload increased? Are you happier at work now than when you first started? Are you happier now than you were this time last year?

The unprecedented number of recent layoffs, particularly of white-collar workers, means the employees who remain have to do more work in the same time to make up for their departed companions, just as the horse did. Trying to do more work in the same time can lead to a stressful work experience. But what choice is there? Nobody dares complain because jobs are scarce. Research shows that more than twenty million Americans are staying in jobs they hate solely because they want to keep their health insurance benefits.

Bureau of Labor statistics show that in households with two parents, both parents work in more than 60 percent of households with children. Home foreclosures have doubled since 1980. Personal bankruptcies have increased 430 percent since 1980. Of the 150 million people currently employed last year, more than 12 million experienced some period of unemployment. Worse, workers today are twice as likely to face a job loss as were their counterparts of the early 1970s. No doubt about it, conditions at work are becoming less secure and more toxic.

What can you do since you can't control economic conditions or single-handedly stop layoffs? "If fate throws a knife at you, there are two ways of catching it—by the blade or by the handle," says an Oriental proverb. You *can* control how you react to the stress and in some cases take active steps to cut down the amount of stress you have to endure. Here are nine steps I've used to C-U-T S-T-R-E-S-S.

Circumvent encounters with stressful people. Don't feel obligated to attend every meeting if it's not required. Select the meetings and discussions that you feel are critical to getting the job done.

Use your time judiciously. Practice time management. Each day, prioritize the tasks that need to be done. Reduce tasks to a manageable number.

Take some time for yourself each day. Take a walk. Listen to music. Exercise. Do a crossword puzzle. Read. Go out to lunch. Meditate. Pray.

Sharpen the saw. Some people are so busy chopping down trees that they forget to make their jobs easier by sharpening the saw. It's Stephen Covey's seventh habit of highly successful people, and it *surrounds* all his other habits. Sharpening the saw is "preserving and enhancing the greatest asset you have—you!" says Covey. Reinvigorate yourself by exercising more, laughing more, sleeping more, and eating better.

Try to negotiate. If the company wants you to work longer hours, ask for a more flexible schedule if it would create less stress for you.

Resign yourself to the fact that things aren't likely to change in the short term. Accept the situation and march on, working "one day at a time."

Explain to your supervisor what you believe are your responsibilities, deadlines, goals, and objectives. Clarify management's expectations, preferably in writing. Update your supervisor regularly—some managers tend to panic when they don't have all the information they need when they need it.

Say no sometimes. Don't be afraid to push back if the demands become overly burdensome. Reiterate what you think your priorities should be. Don't always try to please by simply saying yes.

Seek out support. Ask for help. Delegate to others when possible. Rely on people you can trust.

What can companies do to help employees deal with stress? Identify the most stressful jobs first, and start evaluating ways to make them less stressful if possible. If a particular position is burning out employees quickly, it may be time to redefine the job. Positions that regularly defeat even the best people might be "widow-makers" and require drastic action, says management guru Peter Drucker in *The Essential Drucker.*

Rapid growth or contraction in a company's fortunes can create widow-makers. Sailors coined the term *widow-maker* 150 years ago, referring to New England clipper ships. "When a clipper ship, no matter how well designed or constructed, began to have fatal 'accidents,' the owners did not redesign or rebuild the ship," Drucker says. "They broke it up. Whenever a job defeats two people in a row, who in their earlier assignments had performed well, a company has a widow-maker on its hands." The only solution to this problem, he explains, is to abolish the job.

{
BUSINESS MORAL:
Jobs with excessive demands need to be redefined, shared, or eliminated.
}

SOURCES

Covey, Stephen R. *The 7 Habits of Highly Effective People,* 287. New York: Simon and Schuster, 1989.

Drucker, Peter F. *The Essential Drucker,* 133–34. New York: HarperCollins, 2001.

U.S. Department of Labor. *Employment Characteristics and Families Summary,* 1. USDL 04-719, April 20, 2004.

The Hawk *and* the Pigeons

——————

A hawk had stalked a flock of pigeons for a long time. His plan to swoop down and grab one never worked, though, because the pigeons always saw him coming and fled to safety. The hawk subsequently changed tactics and decided to offer the pigeons a deal.

"Brothers and sisters," the hawk said, "why do you prefer this life of perpetual fear? If you'd promote me to be your king, I could patrol the skies to ensure no one attacks you."

The pigeons discussed the offer, concluded that the hawk possessed special skills in the area of protection that no one else in the flock had, and decided to enthrone him as king. But as soon as the hawk took over as leader, he issued an order that every day, one pigeon would have to be sacrificed for his dinner.

{
AESOP'S MORAL:
Those who willingly put themselves under the power of a despot deserve whatever fate befalls them.
}

PERSPECTIVE: What is your company's approach to promotions? Does it typically promote from within? Are there clear career paths for existing employees to move up through the ranks? Or does your company make a habit of bringing in people from the outside in an effort to infuse the organization with "new blood"?

Companies such as Boeing, Hewlett-Packard, Motorola, Nordstrom, Procter & Gamble, and 3M successfully groomed top managers internally, according to James C. Collins and Jerry I. Porras in *Built to Last: Successful Habits of Visionary Companies.*

They cite General Electric as a stellar example of a company that has successfully promoted from within for more than a hundred years. Jack Welch was only one in a long line of CEOs who transformed GE into the powerhouse that it is today. Gerald Swope (CEO from 1922 to 1939) got GE into the home appliance business. Ralph Cordiner (1950–63) dramatically expanded the number of new markets GE served. Fred Borch (1964–72) moved GE into jet aircraft engines and computers. Reginald Jones (1973–80) expanded GE's fortunes so significantly that a 1980 *U.S. News &World Report* poll listed him as "the most influential person in business today." GE's Crotonville facility serves as the management training and indoctrination center that forges this impressive chain of top-notch talent.

If the situation requires new blood or a fresh look, be careful about the person you bring in. It's possible for an outsider to misrepresent himself as the hawk did, or for company "loyalists" to sabotage the newcomer's efforts. Xerox, Ames, Lucent, Westinghouse, and Zenith went outside the company for new leaders and ended up with less than stellar results. In the case of Xerox, the decision created a financial nightmare.

In 1997, Xerox brought in Richard C. Thoman from IBM as chief operating officer. The decision looked good on paper. Thoman was a thoughtful man, a well-respected strategist, and a protégé of Louis Gerstner while he was at IBM. Xerox wanted change, according to Larry Bossidy and Ram Charan in *Execution: The Discipline of Getting Things Done,* and unfortunately, change was what the company got.

Thoman wasted no time in implementing a series of cost-cutting initiatives. He laid off workers, cut bonuses, trimmed travel budgets, and eliminated perks. When Xerox made him CEO in 1999, Thoman embarked on a radical strategy to transform Xerox from a product and services company into a solutions provider. He formed partnerships with Microsoft and Compaq. His new strategy seemed to energize the lackluster company, and the stock price rose to a record high.

As an outsider, though, Thoman was at a distinct disadvantage because he didn't know one of Xerox's historic weaknesses was its inability to *implement* strategies. Xerox had almost a hundred administration centers that handled accounting, billing, and customer service—an excessive number. Thoman quickly tried to consolidate them into four. Xerox had a sales force of more than thirty thousand people organized by geography instead of service—a big inconsistency for a firm trying to provide customers with solutions and not just hardware. Thoman realigned half the sales force by industry rather than geography. All in all, the changes were too much too soon.

During these transitions, Xerox lost equipment orders, failed to send out invoices, and neglected to answer service calls. The sales force found themselves apologizing to customers and trying to fix the problems. They were so busy putting out fires that they had no time to embrace the new way of selling. Customers grew angrier when the company reassigned sales representatives they had known and trusted for a long time.

Conditions at Xerox deteriorated quickly. Employee morale plummeted, cash flow dried up, and the company's overall financial viability teetered. The stock price went from $64 a share to $7, forcing Xerox to dismiss Thoman in 2000.

In hindsight, the newcomer was doomed from the start. According to Bossidy and Charan, "Xerox's clubby culture did not take kindly to an outsider." How could Thoman have possibly succeeded, let alone chart a new course for the company, when so many people resented his presence and he knew so little about the firm's flaws?

{
BUSINESS MORAL:
*Be wary of bringing in outsiders
for executive positions.*
}

SOURCES

Bossidy, Larry, and Ram Charan. *Execution: The Discipline of Getting Things Done,* 39–41. New York: Crown Business, 2002.

Collins, James C., and Jerry I. Porras. *Built to Last: Successful Habits of Visionary Companies,* 170, 173, 180–82. New York: HarperBusiness, 1994.

The Horse *and* the Groom

A rich man hired a worker to groom his horse. Each day, the worker spent hours brushing the animal but also stole a portion of the horse's allotment of oats and sold them for a profit. The horse's health went downhill rapidly.

Finally, on the verge of collapse, the horse cried out: "If you really want me to be at my best, groom me less and feed me more every day."

{
 AESOP'S MORAL:
A healthy life is lived one day at a time.
}

PERSPECTIVE: How many hours do you typically work each week, including commuting time? Do you feel guilty about not working more? Or do you think you already work too many hours and wish you could cut back? Have you ever worked harder because your company was "grooming" you for a promotion? What do you think drives some of your peers to work as hard as they do? How many workaholics do you know? Overall, how have you maintained a healthy balance between your work and home lives?

Economic pressures are forcing more companies to deny us our daily "oats" to make a little more profit. These oats, which come in the form of time for ourselves and time for our families, are critical to our long-term health. Don't get me wrong, hard work can be beneficial and meaningful. But when hard work, day in, day out, week in, week out, year in, year out, becomes an unyielding crucible of stress, then our health will eventually suffer. Workaholism, it seems, is the only socially acceptable addiction.

In *Working Ourselves to Death,* Diane Fassel describes several dozen characteristics of workaholics. Based on my experiences, the most common ones include:

- *Denial*: A common justification is: "I'm just trying to be a good provider."

- *Multiple addictions*: Some workaholics also have addictions to alcohol, food, or drugs, including cigarettes.

- *Inability to relax*: Even when they're with spouses and families, they can't get the office out of their minds.

- *Obsessiveness*: Perfectionism rules. No job is ever quite good enough and, consequently, ever finished.

- *Self-centeredness*: Work addicts have an exaggerated sense of their own importance and the importance of their work.

- *Spiritual bankruptcy*: If work addicts have no time for themselves and little time for their families, do you think they're going to spend a lot of time getting to know God any better?

If too much work is bad for an individual, having employees work longer hours does not necessarily bring greater productivity to a company, either. Witness what happened to Apple Computer during the 1980s, as described in Geoffrey James's *Business Wisdom of the Electronic Elite.*

When Apple launched the Macintosh, IBM PCs were running an operating system called MS-DOS, a terribly cumbersome Microsoft product. Macintosh was easier to use with its click-on icons—and thus commanded a higher price. Eventually, though, Microsoft's Windows version 3.0 hit the market with a similar Graphical User Interface (GUI). According to James, "Apple could have stolen Microsoft's thunder if it had had the foresight to recode the Macintosh GUI so that it could run on the Intel-based IBM PC." But Apple never made the move. Why did the company stumble? Why could nobody see the glaring opportunity? "The burnout of many Apple employees undoubtedly was a key problem," asserts James.

Apple employees used to sport T-shirts with the motto: "Working 90 hours a week and loving every minute of it." Apple began to expect long hours as the norm and became an unhealthy place to work. "One rumor had it," James says, "that certain managers had begun measuring productivity by the number of divorces in their group—the more divorces, the harder people were working."

During this period, divorce rates in Silicon Valley (where Apple was located) skyrocketed, notes Dennis Hayes in *Behind the Silicon Curtain*. By 1988, almost 65 percent of Apple's employees were in some form of therapy. The company actually made plans to build an on-site psychotherapy facility.

Most workaholics didn't start out sacrificing their lives for the sake of the company. The changeover was gradual, much like the experiment with a frog in a pot of water. If you boil a pot of water and then drop a frog into it, it will immediately jump out. But if you put the frog in a pot of cool water and then gradually raise the temperature to the boiling point, the frog will die.

"Historically, women have been like the canaries in the coal mines, warning of danger," says Judy Beauboeuf, chief legal executive of Barnett Banks, in Virginia O'Brien's *Success on Our Own Terms*. "Women are the first to recognize issues that need attention. Right now, women's voices are being raised around work/life balance issues and they have been its strongest proponents. Like the canaries, they are warning that we were all dying under the stress of not having that balance. I think that's positive and it's influencing what's happening."

{ **BUSINESS MORAL:**
For the long-term health of the company, encourage everybody, especially workaholics, to lead balanced lives. }

SOURCES

Fassel, Diane. *Working Ourselves to Death: The High Cost of Workaholism and the Rewards of Recovery,* 27–29, 38, 109. San Francisco, CA: HarperCollins, 1990.

Hayes, Dennis. *Behind the Silicon Curtain: The Seductions of Work in a Lonely Era,* 116. Boston, MA: South End Press, 1989.

James, Geoffrey. *Business Wisdom of the Electronic Elite: 34 Winning Management Strategies from CEOs at Microsoft, Compaq, Sun, Hewlett-Packard, and Other Top Companies,* 212–13. New York: Times Business/Random House, 1996.

O'Brien, Virginia. *Success on Our Own Terms: Tales of Extraordinary, Ordinary Business Women,* 173. New York: John Wiley & Sons, 1998.

The Lion *and* the Mouse

Amouse ran across the head of a sleeping lion and woke him. With a quick swipe of his paw, the lion scooped up the mouse and roared his displeasure.

"Please don't eat me. I meant no harm," the mouse squeaked. "If you let me go, I'll repay your kindness someday."

The idea of so insignificant a creature ever being able to help the king of beasts so amused the lion that he good-naturedly let the mouse go.

Soon afterward, the lion went prowling for dinner and got caught in a hunter's net. Unable to move, the lion let out a roar of frustration. The mouse heard and recognized the lion's voice, and he scampered to aid the captured beast.

"Your Majesty," the mouse politely said, "let me now be of service to you."

The mouse gnawed at the netting with his tiny teeth until he made a hole big enough for the lion to escape.

{ AESOP'S MORAL:
*No good deed, however
small, is ever wasted.* }

PERSPECTIVE: I began my career in the mail room of our company more than thirty years ago and worked my way up through the organization, eventually becoming a vice president and an officer of the firm. But it was in the mail room, not the boardroom, that I learned a valuable lesson about the value of doing small deeds that served me well throughout my life.

Some employees treated me and the other mail room employees like second-class citizens because "all we did" was deliver mail, make photocopies, and run errands. I felt their disdain: I'm sure they thought, *Once a toady always a toady.* These people had a tendency to talk down to us and treat us like their personal slaves. It was their way of letting us know that we were there only to serve the needs of the engineers and scientists who, according to them, were the important people in the organization. We groaned whenever we saw these people coming.

But other employees treated us with respect, thanked us for our help, and made sure our boss knew what a good job we were doing. Sometimes, they gave us little presents at Christmas. As you might guess, we made extra efforts to assist these people: "You need ten copies of this report by 11:00 a.m. today? No problem." "You need us to work a little later tonight to help you load up presentation materials for a citizens' advisory meeting? We'll be there." It was an easy decision when we had a choice between doing a job for someone who had treated us well versus someone who hadn't.

As I moved up in the organization, I made it a point to acknowledge the support staff in small ways, especially the mail room workers—I never forgot my roots! You can tell what kind of person somebody is by how he treats the person on the lowest rung of your organizational ladder. The people in the company who answer your phones, deliver your mail, make your photocopies, fix your computers, empty your wastebaskets, vacuum your rugs, stock your vending machines, clean your bathrooms, and courier your packages are every bit as deserving of your respect and gratitude as the CEO. It doesn't take much to make the support staff happy, either: a pleasant "thank you," a kind word of praise for a job well done, a short note telling them what good work they do. No small deed is ever wasted.

Sometimes small deeds can make a big difference in an organization—even an organization the size of the U.S. Navy. In *It's Your Ship: Management Techniques from the Best Damn Ship in the Navy,* Captain D. Michael Abrashoff explains how his one small deed created benefits that rippled throughout the entire navy.

Captain Abrashoff commanded the USS *Benfold,* a guided missile destroyer carrying every cutting-edge system the military could provide. When the time came for the sailors' shore leave, the *Benfold* headed for Dubai. Why Dubai? It was one of the only Persian Gulf ports where a crew could get a cold beer in the middle of the searing desert sun. Abrashoff's primary concern, though, as he watched his crew walk down the gangplank toward the city, was safety. Still fresh in his mind was the terrorist detonation at Khobar Towers in 1996 that killed nineteen airmen in Saudi Arabia. Abrashoff had stood in the crater of that blast and resolved that he would do *everything* in his power to protect the lives of his crew.

The captain thought his crew enjoyed the time off in Dubai. He was wrong. They returned to the ship complaining about the buses that shuttled them back and forth. Navy rules required that sailors use local buses to get around—and the men and women hated them. The buses were sixty-passenger dust-filled rattletraps. Worse, the bus drivers were "demons" who refused to stop where the sailors wanted to get off. As he listened to his crew's complaints, Abrashoff realized that there was a bigger problem with the buses than just his crew's discomfort and inconvenience. The rattletraps-posing-as-buses were particularly attractive targets for terrorists who could theoretically kill sixty sailors with one bomb.

Abrashoff decided to reduce the terrorist threat with one small deed. Even though it was against navy rules, he rented twenty vans to drive the sailors around Dubai. Later he argued: "Against regulations or not, it was the right thing to do. Overnight my crew started enjoying Dubai, and I slept better knowing they were safer than before." Abrashoff's small deed made so much sense and was so well appreciated that the navy eventually changed its rule and now routinely uses vans instead of local buses for sailors on leave.

{
BUSINESS MORAL:
Never underestimate the impact of one small deed on your organization.
}

SOURCE

Abrashoff, Captain D. Michael. *It's Your Ship: Management Techniques from the Best Damn Ship in the Navy,* 111–13. New York: Warner Books, 2002.

Winning
Business Strategies

God and business do mix, and profit is a standard
for determining the effectiveness of our combined
efforts. For us, the common link between God and
profit is people.

—C. WILLIAM POLLARD
(FORMER CEO OF SERVICEMASTER)

Let no person . . . presume in prosperity,
for all things are changeable.

—AESOP

The Lion, the Bear, *and* the Fox

A lion and a bear found the carcass of a fawn at the same time. Both were famished, so they began fighting for it. The battle was vicious and continued for some time. Eventually, the animals, bloodied and clawed, fell to the ground half-dead and panting furiously. Neither had the strength to stand up and claim the prize. Just then a fox came by.

Well, look at this, the sly animal said to himself. *These foolish foes have done themselves in, and all for my benefit.*

With that, the fox ran quickly between them, seized the fawn's carcass, and dragged it home.

{
AESOP'S MORAL:
*Only fools fight to exhaustion and
let a rascal make off with the prize.*
}

PERSPECTIVE: Bitter rivals can waste energy trying to gain a slight advantage instead of focusing on what the bigger picture might hold. Competition becomes counterproductive when the inflicted damage is greater than the business benefits. Yet counterproductive battles can create opportunities for third parties to come in and gain an upper hand. That's exactly what Michael Dell did when he saw the two giants Compaq and IBM battling it out in the computer industry, according to Nancy F. Koehn in *Brand New: How Entrepreneurs Earned Customers' Trust from Wedgwood to Dell*.

The year was 1985. Hundreds of companies were making IBM-compatible computers. Most were small start-ups, but one company, Compaq Computer Corporation, was big and getting bigger, and it was giving IBM the biggest run for its money. Compaq took on IBM with spectacular success. Compaq's annual sales reached $500 million by 1988. Like IBM, Compaq decided to use a third-party distribution network to sell its products, so Compaq ended up in many of the same stores where IBM was selling its machines, such as Sears and ComputerLand. Retailers were drawn by Compaq's slightly higher profit margins as well as the fact that Compaq had no direct sales force competing with the retailers' stores. Compaq and IBM continued to battle each other in stores throughout the country.

Enter Michael Dell. Sly like the fox, he watched the two giants waging war, waiting for the right moment to make his move. He decided to develop a different business model and let the giants continue to fight their fight. The problem with IBM and Compaq, he reasoned, was that the workforce selling their computers really didn't know much about the products. Customers buying computers received little technical advice. Dell decided to go with a direct sales model instead of third-party sellers. He based his business plan on having personalized relationships with his customers, letting them specify over the phone exactly what kind of computer they needed.

Koehn explains that the new approach was effective and efficient: "The vast majority of the firm's customers were reached by phone. Most individual customers placed orders by toll-free calls to company salespeople. Once an order was taken, the information was relayed to the company's factory, located close to the [customer's] offices. There, the computer was assembled according to customer specifications."

The customer got exactly what he was looking for, and he had the added advantage of speaking with a knowledgeable computer person who could answer technical questions. The made-to-order or direct sales model also had another major advantage: by eliminating the retailers, that is, the third-party salespeople, Dell was able to cut his distribution costs significantly below his competition's. Dell's customers, once again, received the benefits in the form of lower prices. In 1986, Dell's computers were 30 to 45 percent cheaper than comparable machines offered by IBM or Compaq. In 2002, Dell's annual net revenues exceeded $31 billion. Today the company has 6,700 service people and 50,000 field technicians in 170 countries.

{
BUSINESS MORAL:
Sometimes new opportunities exist even in a fiercely competitive market.
}

SOURCE

Koehn, Nancy F. *Brand New: How Entrepreneurs Earned Customers' Trust from Wedgwood to Dell,* 280–82. Boston, MA: Harvard Business School Press, 2001.

The Fox *and* the Cat

A fox boasted to a cat one day about how sly and wily he was. "I've got all kinds of tricks," the fox said. "For example, whenever I hear the dogs coming, I know a hundred different ways to escape."

The cat was impressed and humbly said, "Your cleverness is amazing. As for me, I have only one way to escape, and that is to climb up a tree. I know it's not as exciting as all of your ways, but it works for me. Maybe someday you could show me some of your different escape routes."

The fox smiled smugly. "Well, friend, perhaps I'll have some free time one of these days, and I can show you a trick or two."

Shortly afterward, the fox and the cat heard a pack of hounds baying nearby.

"They're coming this way!" the cat shrieked.

In a flash, she scaled a nearby tree and hid herself in the leaves. The fox stood there trying to decide which of his many tricks to use. Paralyzed with indecision, the fox waited too long to make his move, and the hounds pounced on him.

{ AESOP'S MORAL:
*One good plan that works is better
than a hundred questionable ones.* }

PERSPECTIVE: Companies invariably strive to grow by moving into new areas of business. The options can be as numerous as the fox's paths of escape. Expanding into new areas or taking a company down new paths, whether related or unrelated to the core businesses, carries inherent risks, especially if it causes the company to neglect its main line of business and profits. If there are any doubts about the planned expansion, it's usually better to stay focused and true to the "one path" that has provided success and then build on that success. Take the case of Dunkin' Donuts.

In *The Winning Performance,* Donald K. Clifford Jr. and Richard E. Cavanagh describe how the highly successful coffee company went wrong for a while. Founded in 1950 by William Rosenberg in Quincy, Massachusetts, the company was still thriving five years later, building new donut shops each month. Then Rosenberg decided to expand into new areas. Dunkin' Donuts started a drive-in hamburger chain called Howdy's. It began providing food to institutions and stocking vending machines. It went into fish and chips, and thought seriously about hats and educational programs—in effect, any type of business that could be franchised.

The diversification began to fail. For five years, Rosenberg neglected the all-important coffee business, and profits suffered. His attention was too spread out over too many initiatives to be effective. Rosenberg and his partner, Tom Schwarz, got back to basics; they sold off all of the businesses except coffee—the path that had always worked for them before. Dunkin' Donuts focused on becoming the best at serving coffee and donuts.

The company set out to provide, to management's thinking, the best cup of coffee in the world. "Dunkin' Donuts has a twenty-three-page specification of what it requires in a coffee bean," say Clifford and Cavanagh. "Beans are to be used within ten days of their delivery; if they are not, they are returned on the next Dunkin' Donuts' supply truck. Once the coffee is brewed, it can be served for only eighteen minutes; after that it must be thrown out. And the coffee must be brewed between 196 and 198 degrees Fahrenheit exactly." By 1984, the company had 1,350 shops around the world. Today it has more than 5,000.

"The most profitable businesses over long periods of time are single-product businesses in the right product, the IBMs, the GMs," observes Peter Drucker in *Managing in Turbulent Times*. "A conglomerate, on the other hand, being an assembly, under one management of a wide diversity of businesses without a common core of unity, cannot expect superior results and performance in the long run, and especially not in turbulent times."

{ BUSINESS MORAL: *Don't be distracted from what you do best.* }

SOURCES

Clifford, Donald K., Jr., and Richard E. Cavanagh. *The Winning Performance: How America's High-Growth Midsize Companies Succeed*, 65–66. New York: Bantam Books, 1985.

Drucker, Peter F. *Managing in Turbulent Times*, 65. New York: HarperBusiness, 1993.

The Fox *and* the Lion

A fox scurrying through the woods stopped short when he saw a lion coming down the same path from the opposite direction. Before his enemy could strike, the frightened fox bolted into the deeper forest. Stopping to catch his breath, the fox turned around anxiously to see if the lion was pursuing him. In fact, the king of beasts had continued down the path, enjoying the fine day.

Sometime later, the fox and the lion met on the same path. But this time, the fox contained his fear and stepped aside to let the majestic beast pass.

"Good morning," the fox politely said.

"A good morning to you," replied the lion.

The third time the two met, the fox felt no fear, and he asked the lion about the health of his family.

{
AESOP'S MORAL:
*You tend to fear opponents less as
you get to know them better.*
}

PERSPECTIVE: Who are your top five competitors? How does your firm stack up against them? Are your competitors bigger than you? Or are they smaller firms trying to take away niche markets? Is the competition with other companies friendly? Or is it a cutthroat, win-at-any-cost battle royal? Has your CEO ever collaborated with any of the CEOs from your competitors? Can you conceive of any situation where you might want to team up with or get closer to one of your competitors?

"There are many things my father taught me here in this room," Michael Corleone says in *The Godfather: Part II*. "He taught me: keep your friends close, but your enemies closer."

In the engineering industry, competitors routinely join forces on large projects. Why? Two reasons. The first is the expected value of the payback. Fifty percent of a large project is better than one hundred percent of nothing if the client doesn't happen to select your company. The second reason is synergy. Firm A may have local business relationships in a city bidding out a large project, but may be weak in one or two technical areas required by the contract. Consequently, Firm A may team up with Firm B, a competitor who does not have a local presence, but is well regarded in the technical areas where Firm A is weak. Firm B agrees to sign the teaming arrangement because it wants to expand operations in that city. By teaming, the firms assemble a powerful force capable of meeting every criterion for selection, and become almost unbeatable. Even better, the companies won't have to compete against each other on this particular project as they have so often in other parts of the country. For the most part, the engineering firms that team up tend to be equal in size and stature and differ only in the expertise they bring and the knowledge of the potential client.

But what happens if your competitors are much bigger than you? Can any good come out of working with your competition under those conditions? Can a small firm ever offer anything different from or better than a larger firm? In *How to Drive Your Competition Crazy*, Guy Kawasaki describes a classic David versus Goliath story between Bob Curry, owner of a small hardware store in Quincy, Massachusetts, and the corporate behemoth Home Depot.

Bob Curry learned that Home Depot was opening a megastore one quarter of a mile from his small store. He figured out that the key to survival was service—there was no way an enormous store with 150 employees and 120,000 square feet of shelf space could know customers the way that his employees could. He developed niche markets such as filling propane tanks and servicing power tools. He kept his prices competitive and publicized his long-standing partnerships with local groups such as the Rotary Club.

One day, the Home Depot manager in charge of power tools came into Curry's store to see how well the small shop served its customers. The manager was so amazed by the smaller store's level of service that he felt comfortable sending Home Depot customers down to Curry's for items and services that Home Depot didn't provide.

Bob Curry explains,

He told us that from now on they're going to send anyone with any kind of a service problem to us. Customers who buy a gas grill at Home Depot ask employees where they can get propane. Home Depot sends them right down to us. Hopefully, we capture them as customers. We make the customers go in the store to pay for the propane, which is stored outside, so they're forced to learn more about us. We work hard to build some kind of bond between Home Depot and us rather than try to fight. If Home Depot wanted to, it could swallow us up.

Curry spoke those words almost ten years ago. I wondered whether his informal arrangement with Home Depot was still in effect. Bob's store and the Home Depot are both fifteen miles from my home, so last month I visited the stores to see whether Home Depot was still recommending Bob's store for propane refills and whether Bob's service was still as good as ever. Actually, I had a third goal: to buy a package of 100-watt lightbulbs. Let me tell you how my trip went.

First, I walked into Home Depot, a mammoth building stacked to its cavernous ceilings with merchandise. I wanted lightbulbs, so naturally I went to the Lighting Department, located at the very back of the store. I couldn't find what I was looking for so I asked a salesclerk for help. "What you want is in a display at the front of the store," he said.

I walked to the front of the store. I saw the display, but it had no 100-watt bulbs. I asked a clerk up front for assistance. "You'll find our 100-watt bulbs in the Lighting Department," she told me. I walked to the back of the store again. The original salesclerk was gone, and a new one had taken his place. I asked him for assistance. "I don't see any 100-watt bulbs here. You'd better go to the front of the store and ask at the Help Desk."

By then, I had frittered away fifteen minutes of my precious life. Enough was enough. As I left the store, lightbulb-less, I asked a cashier where I could get propane for a new tank. "Curry's Hardware, right down the street," she replied.

I pulled into Curry's small parking lot. As I got out of my car, a salesclerk stationed outside for propane refills came over to me and pleasantly asked me what I needed.

"A package of 100-watt lightbulbs," I replied.

"As you walk in the front door, the 100-watt bulbs will be in the second aisle on the right," he assured me. I found them right where he said I would.

As I went back to my car with my purchase, this same fellow asked me: "Do you need a propane tank refilled today?"

"Not today," I said.

"Then have a great day and we'll see you again soon," he told me.

I drove home with everything I wanted to know. Yes, Home Depot still refers customers to Curry's, and, yes, Curry's customer service remains outstanding. And if you ever find yourself in Quincy looking for 100-watt lightbulbs, I know just the place to go.

{
BUSINESS MORAL:
Sometimes it makes sense to find ways to work with the competition.
}

SOURCE

Kawasaki, Guy. *How to Drive Your Competition Crazy: Creating Disruption for Fun and Profit,* 157, 159, 161–63. New York: Hyperion, 1995.

The Wolf in Sheep's Clothing

A hungry wolf stalked a flock of sheep but couldn't grab one because a dutiful shepherd watched over them. Finding a discarded sheepskin, the wolf placed it over his own fur and slowly crept into the middle of the flock without the shepherd noticing. Instead of pouncing on the nearest lamb and making his escape, the wolf decided to wait until nighttime when the flock was locked up and the shepherd was eating supper.

Then I'll have my pick of the flock, the wolf thought, *enjoy a most delicious meal, and slip away unseen.*

But that evening, the shepherd decided to have a big supper before retiring. He went to the sheep pen in the dark, reached in, and grabbed the first sheep he put his hands on—which turned out to be the wolf—and killed him.

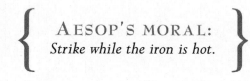

{ AESOP'S MORAL:
Strike while the iron is hot. }

PERSPECTIVE: "The best is the enemy of the good," said General George S. Patton. "By this I mean a good plan violently executed now is better than a perfect plan next week." Unfortunately, the perfect plan is usually the goal of many business managers, according to Warren J. Ridge in *Follow Me! Business Leadership Patton Style.* And in many cases, the timeline of opportunity does not allow waiting until all the information is in or all of the bugs have been worked out.

Ridge describes how Patton believed that Field Marshal Montgomery missed many chances to attack and exploit the enemy's position during World War II because he usually waited for the perfect plan and the perfect moment. Both generals were trying to take the strategic city of Messina during the Sicilian invasion, with Montgomery pushing north, and Patton dashing westward along the coast. Capturing Messina would open the gate to the Allied invasion of Italy.

The Germans' antitank traps were formidable, but Patton kept advancing. Montgomery, by contrast, started to hold back to collect more information for his advance. The Germans fought stubbornly, but realized they were losing control and began to evacuate soldiers across the Strait of Messina into Italy. According to Ridge, as Patton neared Messina, he sent a five-gallon jerry can of gasoline back to Monty with the message: "Although sadly short of gasoline myself, I know of your admiration for our equipment, and can spare you this five gallons. It will be more than enough to take you as far as you will probably advance in the next two days."

Patton beat Montgomery to Messina. By August 17, 1943, the entire island was in Allied hands.

War often creates urgencies requiring bold action with less-than-perfect plans. This isn't always the case in business. Have you ever heard the saying "The early bird gets the worm, but the second mouse in gets the cheese"? Depending on how much risk a company wants to avoid, it may be more prudent to wait until more information is available before embarking on a new venture. More planning is not necessarily "nondoing." Maybe a company has a plan that is almost complete, but the timing isn't right (the economy is soft, for example). Maybe with a few more test runs, a company can eradicate all of the bugs in a product. Procter & Gamble is renowned for making every test imaginable before unveiling a new product. The information-gathering and testing process takes longer but greatly reduces the risk of the initiative. P&G has few failures once it decides to launch something new.

Some companies combine a "wait and attack" approach. They hold back until a competitor develops a new product, and then they move in quickly for the kill. The term *creative imitation* sounds like an oxymoron, but it refers to a strategy whereby a company waits for somebody else to establish a new product or service—but only approximately. Then the company moves as quickly as Patton to come out with the exact new product or service the customer really wants. The creative imitation then becomes the standard and dominates the market.

Management guru Peter Drucker describes how Japan's Hattori Company used this strategy to dominate the watch industry. As semiconductors became increasingly available, people in the industry began to realize the potential to make watches that were more accurate, more reliable, and less expensive. The Swiss, who long dominated the world of timepieces, had developed a quartz-powered digital watch. But because of their history in manufacturing traditional timepieces, the Swiss decided to introduce the new line of watches very gradually—making them, in effect, luxury items.

"Meanwhile," Drucker says, "the Hattori Company had long been making conventional watches for the Japanese market. It saw the opportunity and went in for creative imitation, developing the quartz-powered watch as the standard timepiece. By the time the Swiss had awakened, it was too late. Seiko watches had become the world's best sellers, with the Swiss almost pushed out of the market." The strategy can be risky if companies misread the trends or creatively imitate a product that turns out to be *not* what the customer wants.

So which is the better approach: to march in boldly or wait until the time is right? No strategy is foolproof, but timely action is usually better than patient inaction, as long as a company acknowledges and accepts the risks and costs associated with failure.

{
BUSINESS MORAL:
A good plan executed today is better than a perfect one that's too late.
}

SOURCES

Drucker, Peter F. *Managing in Turbulent Times,* 65. New York: HarperBusiness, 1993.

Ridge, Warren J. *Follow Me! Business Leadership Patton Style,* 24. New York: AMACOM, 1989.

The Ant *and* the Grasshopper

A grasshopper chirped loudly during the heat of a summer's day. An ant warned the grasshopper that it would be winter before long, and that he should begin thinking about the cold times ahead. The grasshopper ignored the ant and kept on singing, thinking only of his short-term pleasure. The ant, by contrast, spent the rest of the summer gathering kernels of wheat and storing them for the colder months. The winter was an especially bitter one, and one night the cold and starving grasshopper approached the ant for something to eat.

"What did you do all summer while I was gathering food?" the ant asked.

"Oh, I was busy too," replied the grasshopper. "I sang all day long."

Unmoved, the ant said sternly: "Because you decided to sing all summer, it looks like you'll have to dance all winter."

{
AESOP'S MORAL:
*It is wise to prepare today
for the needs of tomorrow.*
}

PERSPECTIVE: What is your company's planning horizon? Five years? Two years? Six months? Does your company often set aside its long-term vision to meet shorter-term financial goals? Companies are under enormous pressure to deliver bottom-line results every quarter. The pressures can rearrange a company's priorities, and sometimes not for the better.

For many years, I was fortunate to have worked for a firm that was owned by its employees. Our stockholders weren't anonymous and remote investors interested only in short-term payback, but workers intimately involved with our company's business and committed to its long-term success. Because the company's stock was not publicly traded, we had more freedom to plan for the future. Believe me, we all knew that the company had to make a profit. But because we weren't obliged to provide huge dividends every quarter, we were able to reinvest some of those profits for longer-term initiatives.

Large international conglomerates bought many of our competitors. Their planning horizons shortened overnight. They let talented people go because the markets those people specialized in happened to be flat at the time. Management didn't have the patience to wait until the markets came back, which they usually did. In some cases, the companies lost so many people that their technical expertise was never the same again.

How important is it to maintain a long-term planning horizon? W. Edwards Deming had strong opinions on the subject. Deming became one of the great post–World War II business leaders. He has been credited with turning the Japanese economy around after the war. In *Out of the Crisis*, Deming outlined his fourteen principles to transform management in the Western world. His very first principle deals with having the vision to plan for tomorrow.

He identified two types of problems: those of today and those of tomorrow. It is easy for companies to get caught up in the problems of today, such as maintaining product quality, sales, profits, public relations, and so on. But he noted that the problems of the future are the problems that should "command first and foremost constancy of purpose, and dedication to improvement of competitive position," because these things will keep the company going for the next ten, twenty, or thirty years.

Vision will lead to innovation, and innovation will lead to constantly improving designs for products and services. Deming explained, "It is a mistake to suppose that efficient production of a product and service can with certainty keep an organization solvent and ahead of competition. It is possible and, in fact, fairly easy for an organization to go downhill and out of business making the wrong product or offering the wrong type of service, even though everyone in the organization performs with devotion, employing statistical methods and every other aid that can boost efficiency."

Deming believed it was the role of management to create a constancy of purpose and a vision for the future. He did *not* consider rolling out next quarter's sales targets as vision.

> { BUSINESS MORAL:
> *Long-term planning is the key*
> *to survival and success.* }

SOURCE

Deming, W. Edwards. *Out of the Crisis,* 24–26. Cambridge, MA: Massachusetts Institute of Technology, Center for Advanced Engineering Study, 1986.

The Farmer *and* His Sons

A farmer, on the verge of death, called his two sons to him: "My good and grateful sons, I'm not long for this world. Everything that I leave to you can be found in our vineyard."

The old man passed away soon afterward. Thinking that their father had left a great treasure for them in the vineyard, his sons began to energetically explore it. Using spades and plows, they turned over every last bit of earth. They knew all parts of the vineyard and examined every plant. Eventually, they realized that there was, in fact, no great treasure. But because of the thorough spade work, the vines strengthened, the harvest grew richer, and the wine the brothers made that year was the best vintage ever.

{
AESOP'S MORAL:
Industry sometimes creates surprise dividends.
}

PERSPECTIVE: How much do you know about your company and the business you're in? Is your knowledge limited to the division you work in, the product or service you offer, or the function you perform? Do you know how your company makes money? Most of us are so busy trying to do our own jobs that we don't have a lot of extra time to learn what other groups in the organization do. Yet a company can develop clear and measurable advantages when its employees know the business as well as the farmer's sons knew the vineyard.

Let me share with you a personal story of how a company's effectiveness can improve the more employees know about the business. Margaret was one of our switchboard operators in the days before direct dialing. Our office had seven hundred employees, so she and her coworkers were always busy fielding incoming calls. Margaret was exactly the type of person you'd want answering the phone: warm and upbeat with a pleasant voice. She took a call one day from a potential client, although she didn't know that at the time.

"I'd like to speak to the person who handles proposals for hazardous waste work in your company," the man said.

"I don't know who that is," Margaret replied. "You'll have to give me a name."

"I don't know the name. That's the point," the man said. "Listen. I'm the contract administrator for my company. All I know is that my boss told me to send your firm a proposal because we want you to bid on an important job with a short deadline."

Margaret couldn't help him. "I'm sorry," she said nicely. "But you need to give me a name."

The conversation went back and forth like that for several minutes until the frustrated caller hung up. How did I know this conversation ever took place? A week later, a friend who worked for one of our competitors called me to alert me about the problem. "You guys missed out on a great opportunity," he said. He then described how he attended a pre-bid meeting with other firms interested in the job. The contract administrator chaired the meeting and related our switchboard story to everyone in the room.

Ouch. The project was a big one, and our firm would have liked the chance to work for this Fortune 500 company. I called the contract administrator and apologized on behalf of our firm. He graciously accepted my apology and advised: "You only get one chance to make a good first impression with me."

Was this missed opportunity Margaret's fault? Absolutely not. It was management's fault for not training her properly. I met with my supervisor to discuss the incident. Within two days, Margaret and other key support staff attended a short training session that gave them important information about the different organizations within the company. Margaret and all subsequent switchboard operators now have a list of people to route a call to, depending on what the caller wants, be it someone from marketing, operations, payroll, or engineering.

It's especially critical that receptionists and the people who answer your phones know your business because they are often the first employees that your customers meet or talk to. Disney understands that one of the first employees you meet in the theme parks is the ticket taker, so the company trains its ticket takers to provide answers to commonly asked questions when people enter the parks, such as what time the parade starts, where the restrooms are, and how often the shuttle buses run.

A company should seek to develop leaders at every level, not just managers, says management expert Warren Bennis in *On Becoming a Leader*. He cites Robert Townsend, the person who turned around Avis car rental. Townsend insisted that every executive know the car rental business in depth. "Every Avis executive was required to don the Avis red jacket," Bennis says, "and work at the company checkout stations regularly." The German composer and conductor Gustav Mahler required every member of his symphony orchestra to sit out in the audience at regular intervals to understand how things looked and sounded from the audience's viewpoint. This hands-on knowledge of a business helps employees buy into the overall vision of the company.

According to Bennis, a firm's vision of itself falls into three categories: strategic, tactical, and personal. *Strategic* vision involves a firm's definition of itself and where it fits in the marketplace. *Tactical* vision focuses on the way the firm implements that strategic vision. *Personal* vision encompasses the way in which that strategic vision is made manifest in each and every employee.

"If you want to measure the effectiveness of, say, a retail operation, measure the attitude of any clerk in any store," Bennis advises. "If the clerk is rude, unknowledgeable, helpless, chances are the top executives are either inept or lack a coherent vision." The more employees know about a business, the more empowered they feel, the greater their productivity, and the more opportunities for them to demonstrate their leadership qualities.

Job rotation is another way a company can help employees learn more about the business and broaden their personal vision. Chubb Insurance's managers expand their company knowledge through job rotation. In *Success on Our Own Terms,* Virginia O'Brien describes how one Chubb employee, Jan Tomlinson, started out as an underwriter but then rotated into Human Resources (HR). O'Brien explains why it was a great move: "As teamwork is becoming more critical to the efficiency and effectiveness of work processes, the human element, and therefore, the HR function, is becoming more important to business strategy."

Through her HR rotation, Jan deepened her knowledge of the company, broadened her skills, enlarged her network, and widened her global perspective. She eventually became president of Chubb Insurance Company of Canada. Jan says: "You can go one of two ways: You can either burrow yourself at your desk or you can spend as much time as you possibly can learning about the world around you."

{ BUSINESS MORAL:
*Encourage all employees to
know the business inside and out.* }

SOURCES

Bennis, Warren G. *On Becoming a Leader,* 183–86. Reading, MA: Addison-Wesley Publishing Company, 1989.

O'Brien, Virginia. *Success on Our Own Terms: Tales of Extraordinary, Ordinary Business Women,* 108–10. New York: John Wiley & Sons, 1998.

The Eagle *and* the Beetle

A hare fleeing an eagle scampered to a beetle's nest and asked for protection. The beetle tried to hide the hare, but the eagle had a keen eye and grabbed him.

The beetle pleaded for the hare's release: "I gave this hare refuge, and I respectfully ask you not to violate the law of sanctuary."

The eagle sneered at the little bug, swatted him aside, and flew off to her nest to eat the hare. The beetle, seething, decided to learn as much as he could about his feathered enemy. As the eagle flew away, the beetle followed the bird to her nest. The beetle tracked the comings and goings of the eagle for several days until he figured out the bird's hunting schedule. Waiting until the eagle flew off one day, the beetle flew up to the nest and rolled the eagle's eggs out, one by one. The eggs splattered when they hit the ground.

When the eagle returned to the nest and saw her smashed eggs, she was furious: "Who would commit such an outrageous act?"

To prevent the same thing from happening, she built a nest in a taller tree. But again, the beetle tracked her movements, returned to the nest, and destroyed the eggs. Desperate, the eagle flew up to Jupiter and begged the god to take the third brood of eggs, place it on his lap, and protect it, which the god consented to do. But the beetle formed a little dust ball, carried it up to the god, and dropped it in his lap. When Jupiter saw the piece of dust, he rose to shake it off, dropping and breaking the third brood of eggs.

Jupiter soon realized what the beetle had done. Fearing that eagles would become extinct if the feud continued, he approached the beetle about a truce. The insect refused to cooperate, forcing the god to move all eagles' breeding time to another season, when no beetles are about.

{ AESOP'S MORAL:
*Never underestimate the power
of an enemy with resolve.* }

PERSPECTIVE: How well do you know your competition? Does your company regularly collect information on what your competitors are up to? How does your company get information about your competitors? Gathering and applying competitive intelligence could make your company more successful and, in extreme cases, could be crucial to its survival.

Competitive intelligence is *not* stealing another company's trade secrets or sending in spies to illegally collect "dirt" on a firm. Competitive intelligence *is* using readily available information about a specific company or group of companies to learn more about how they do business: How did they perform financially last year? What staff changes have they made? What new products have they unveiled? What alliances have they formed with other companies? Where are they opening new offices? What are their market strategies?

Collecting information is amazingly easy using the Internet. Here are just a few online sources available at your fingertips:

- Company Web sites

- Vendor Web sites

- Security and Exchange Commission filings

- Trade and industry associations and publications
- Conference proceedings
- Newspaper articles
- Employment ads
- Patent and trademark filings
- Demographic data

As was the case for the beetle, the more you know about your competitors, the better you'll be able to craft a successful strategy to come out ahead of them. "The most valuable lessons of all are learned from your competitors," says Al Kaltman. In his book *Cigars, Whiskey and Winning: Leadership Lessons from General Ulysses S. Grant*, he describes how Grant used his competitive intelligence during an important Civil War battle.

Grant got to know many of the people he would command or oppose during the Civil War when he fought alongside them in the Mexican War years earlier. He believed his experiences helped him understand the strategies those men would later use. In February 1862, Grant decided to capture Fort Donelson, a fifteen-acre Confederate fortification located strategically on a bluff overlooking the Cumberland River in Tennessee. The rebels fought fiercely and fended off Grant's first attack, but they were hemmed in and knew they'd eventually have to make a move.

The two men in command of the fort, General John Floyd and his second, General Gideon Pillow, discussed their options and decided their only course of action was to try a breakout at dawn. All night long, the rebels shifted troops to Pillow's sector. The morning of February 15, 1862, was bitterly cold with howling winds and falling snow. The rebels attacked and surprised the Union regiments. Who'd expect an attack in such weather? Grant was miles downstream of the fighting, conferring on war strategies with Flag Officer Andrew Foote.

The Union commander at Fort Donelson sent a message to Grant telling him of the surprise attack. By the time Grant reached Fort Donelson, the Union troops were in disarray, and the rebels had broken through one of the biggest Union lines and were about to escape through the breach.

Grant refused to panic. Deciding not to wait for reinforcements, he ordered his men to counterattack the heavily entrenched enemy force and seal the breach. Why did Grant make such a brazen and courageous move? He knew Gideon Pillow personally from the Mexican War days, and he had nothing but contempt for the man, thinking him "conceited" and an ineffective general. If he forcefully staunched the flow through the breach immediately, Grant decided, his old acquaintance would get a case of the shies and withdraw to the fort to regroup. He wasted no time going directly at Pillow.

In his memoirs, Grant wrote that because he knew Pillow and his reticence so well, he "judged that with any force, no matter how small, I could march up within gunshot of any entrenchments he was given to hold."

Pillow's men fell back. The breakout failed. Grant had retrapped the Confederate force. Inside the fort, the commanders once again discussed their options. Pillow wanted to try another breakout, but Floyd and General Simon Buckner convinced him that 75 percent of the men would die in the next attempt. The group decided surrender was the only answer, but neither Floyd nor Pillow wanted to be the person to do it. Floyd commandeered two steamboats and sneaked down the river with fifteen hundred troops. Pillow climbed into a skiff and rowed to the other side of the Cumberland River and escaped. Only Buckner decided to stay with his men and endure whatever fate befell them.

Buckner sent a proposal to Grant with terms of surrender. Grant's reply became famous: "No terms except an unconditional and immediate surrender can be accepted." Buckner had no choice but to capitulate.

With this victory, the Union army captured fifteen thousand Confederate prisoners, controlled the Cumberland and Tennessee Rivers, and kept the rebels out of Kentucky. Grant went from clerk to hero overnight. Newspapers admiringly reported that the U.S. in his name stood for Unconditional Surrender.

After the surrender, Grant had a conversation with Buckner, his old friend who had loaned him money many times before the war. "He said to me that if he had been in command, I would not have got up to Donelson as easily as I did," Grant recalled. "I told him that if he had been in command, I should have not tried it in the way I did."

Study your competition. Observe their weaknesses. Learn from their mistakes. Understand what they might be doing better than you. Build on any good ideas they have. Sam Walton of Wal-Mart made it a practice to personally study the competition. He would carry a tape recorder and make notes about pricing strategies and marketing ideas while strolling around competitors' stores. Kmart's Harry Cunningham said, "From the time anybody first noticed Sam, it was obvious he had adopted almost all of the original Kmart ideas. I always had great admiration for the way he implemented—and later enlarged on—those ideas."

{
BUSINESS MORAL:
Constantly figure out what it takes to get ahead of your competition . . . and stay there.
}

SOURCES

Kaltman, Al. *Cigars, Whiskey and Winning: Leadership Lessons from General Ulysses S. Grant,* 55–56. Paramus, NJ: Prentice Hall Press, 1998.

Walton, Sam. *Sam Walton: Made in America,* 191. New York: Doubleday, 1992.

Business Strategies That Failed

Do not look where you fell, but where you slipped.

—AFRICAN PROVERB

Take heed of that vulgar error, of thinking that there is anything good in evil. It is a mistake when people talk of profitable knavery, or of starving honesty; for virtue and justice carry all that is good and profitable with them.

—AESOP

The Eagle *and* the Fox

An eagle and a fox shared the same tree for many years. The eagle built her nest in the treetop, while the fox made her home in a hole in the giant roots below. One day the eagle decided to take advantage of her high-altitude home. She waited for the fox to go out and then swooped down, grabbed one of the young kits, and flew back to her nest. She was all set to devour the juicy kit when the fox returned.

"What do you think you're doing?" the fox cried up to the eagle. "What about our friendship? Give me back my child at once."

But the eagle ignored the fox's plea. She was sure that her own little birds were too high up for the fox to grab them. When the fox realized that the eagle was not going to relent, she raced to a nearby altar where a fire was still burning. Grabbing a flaming stick, the fox hurried back to the bottom of the tree. The eagle quickly realized that the fox meant to set fire to the tree and burn her and her little birds into ashes.

"Wait a minute!" the eagle shouted down to the fox. "I'll bring your kit back to you at once."

{
AESOP'S MORAL:
*It is sometimes necessary
to fight fire with fire.*
}

97

PERSPECTIVE: Sometimes the scorched earth approach is the only one that will work, according to Avinash Dixit and Barry Nalebuff in *Thinking Strategically*. They cite Houghton Mifflin, the publishing house, as a firm that successfully used the fox's strategy to thwart a hostile takeover by Western Pacific. Houghton Mifflin threatened to empty its stable of authors if Western Pacific continued to push the sale through. At the time, John Kenneth Galbraith, Archibald MacLeish, Arthur Schlesinger Jr., and many other authors of moneymaking textbooks were under contract to Houghton Mifflin. All threatened to quit if the acquisition moved forward. Western Pacific's chairman, Howard Newman, thought the gambit was a bluff at first, but he slowly realized it wasn't as each author in turn sent him a letter confirming his planned resignation. Newman concluded that there would be nothing left of Houghton Mifflin if the deal went through. Western Pacific withdrew its offer, and Houghton Mifflin remained independent.

This strategy doesn't always work, as Rupert Murdoch knew when he decided to buy *New York,* the modern city-life magazine founded by Clay Felker and Milton Glaser in 1968. Murdoch pursued the deal, even though many of the magazine's better-known writers threatened to leave if the acquisition proceeded. Murdoch completed the deal anyway, and the writers quit. The advertisers, however, had already decided to stay. And Murdoch wanted the advertisers. He assumed that it would be much easier to get new writers—the previous writers weren't *that* well known. Dixit and Nalebuff explain, "The writers burned the wrong fields. For the scorched earth strategy to be effective, you must destroy what the invader wants, which may not coincide with what the present occupants value."

The fox, by contrast, knew quite well that the eagle would give in.

{
BUSINESS MORAL:
*The scorched earth approach to a
hostile takeover works only if you threaten
to burn what the other side wants.*
}

SOURCE

Dixit, Avinash, and Barry Nalebuff. *Thinking Strategically: The Competitive Edge in Business, Politics and Everyday Life,* 119–20. New York: W. W. Norton and Company, 1993.

The Eagle *and* the Crow

A crow saw an eagle flying amid the highest treetops.

I can do that, the crow said to herself.

Next, the eagle swiftly dived to earth and then landed softly next to a brook to get a drink.

What a show-off! I can get a drink the same way, the crow thought.

The eagle then soared into the sky and swooped down and pounced on a little lamb grazing in a field. The eagle's strong wings bore him and the lamb aloft until they reached the eagle's nest.

The crow thought, *That's surely the easiest way to get dinner.*

Seeing a ram off to the side, the crow swooped down and tried to pick him up and carry him off. She dug her claws into the ram's wool and tugged, but the ram didn't budge. Instead, the crow got tangled in the ram's wool.

The shepherd heard the crow's squawking. *What's that terrible racket?* he wondered.

He looked over and saw the crow frantically trying to free herself from the ram's wool. The shepherd captured the bird, clipped her wings, and brought her home in a cage.

{ **AESOP'S MORAL:**
*It takes more than just
wings to be an eagle.* }

PERSPECTIVE: What does it take to be an eagle? Can you remember examples of when you or your firm tried to push your limits to achieve greater success? What happened? How fine a line do you think there is between confidence and overconfidence?

My wife was a manager for Federated Department Stores for five years during the early 1980s. The companies under the Federated banner had been in business for many years, were well regarded, and consistently made money. But in the high-flying 1980s, the fortunes of Federated changed markedly because one man's overconfidence ran amok. In *The 10 Dumbest Mistakes Smart People Make and How to Avoid Them,* Arthur Freeman and Rose DeWolf describe what happened when Albert Campeau committed the sin of "believing his own press agent."

Campeau made his name and his fortune building homes. He thought it would be a cinch to transfer his success to another venture. The Canadian borrowed more than $9 billion so that he could take over Federated Department Stores and Allied Department Stores, another huge retail chain with a long-standing reputation and track record of success. The fact was, Campeau knew absolutely nothing about the retail business. He convinced himself that a lack of experience wouldn't really stop him from becoming successful.

But the financial realities were stark: the interest Campeau was paying on debt was greater than the largest pretax profits Federated and Allied had ever made in their history. Like the crow, Campeau had taken on more than he could handle. And like the crow, his wings were clipped. Campeau acquired Federated and Allied on April Fools' Day, 1988. By 1990, both companies were bankrupt, and Campeau was no longer in control.

When things are going well, it is natural to maintain confidence and think that things will continue to go well. Confidence and positive thinking are generally viewed as assets. But both need to be tempered with the occasional reality check.

{
BUSINESS MORAL:
*Don't let your ego convince you
to take on more than you can handle.*
}

SOURCE

Freeman, Dr. Arthur M., and Rose DeWolf. *The 10 Dumbest Mistakes Smart People Make and How to Avoid Them,* 83, 85. New York: HarperCollins, 1992.

The Frog *and* the Ox

Two little frogs saw an amazing sight and quickly hopped home to tell their father.

"Father," the first frog said, "we saw the biggest and most terrible monster in the world. It was huge, had horns on its head, a long tail, hooves—"

The father interrupted his child: "Why, it was no monster. It was an ox. And I don't think it was that big. In fact, I bet I could make myself as big as an ox if I tried."

With that, the father puffed himself out. "Was he as big as I am now?" he asked.

"He was much bigger," the little frogs said.

The father made himself grow even bigger. "Was he this big?" he asked again.

"Bigger, Father. He was much, much bigger!"

The father frog grew still bigger until—*Pop!*—he burst into pieces.

{
AESOP'S MORAL:
Self-conceit can lead to self-destruction.
}

PERSPECTIVE: Most companies want to expand and grow. Growth can boost revenues, increase geographical coverage, enhance capabilities, and create more opportunities for employees to move up the organizational ladder. How fast is your company growing? Have you seen additional opportunities for yourself? What special problems do you think growth can cause?

Although just about every businessperson believes growing is critical to a company's long-term survival, companies can grow too fast and get too big for their own good and end up in pieces like the frog. Don Burr, founder of People's Express Airline, had grand plans to grow his company as big as possible. In *Competitive Advantage Through People*, Jeffrey Pfeffer describes what happened when the airline tried to grow too big too quickly.

People's Express was an almost overnight success in the early 1980s. The airline acted quickly and aggressively once the federal government deregulated the industry. Its workers gave the airline a significant competitive advantage. How? People's Express deliberately selected and trained its workforce to be the best in the business. The talent assembled by the airline proved to be a catalyst for its initial growth.

Everybody loved People's Express. Business schools across America used it as a case study. Newspapers and magazines printed highly complimentary articles. Television programs like *20/20* held up the company as an example of how to successfully grow a business. It was all too good to be true. The advantage that company had when it first started out eventually became a major impediment to its survival.

People's Express routinely screened one hundred applicants to find one new trainee. An applicant lucky enough to make the cut then attended five weeks of unpaid training. All this, and there was still no guarantee of being hired! Once trained, applicants still had one more hurdle to jump: score at least 90 percent on a company test. Then, and only then, did People's Express deem a trainee qualified to join the organization. Once on board, new hires attended still more training programs aimed at creating self-managed teams.

The airline's screening and training process was comprehensive. It was also time-consuming, expensive, and in the end, totally incompatible with a company growing as fast as People's Express was.

Sunny skies darkened. The airline hit turbulence. Its stellar workforce, the engine that powered its ascent, began to burn out. Illness and divorce rates took off. Morale nosedived. What was "Captain" Don Burr's response? Grow bigger faster. It was inevitable that the company's stock price wouldn't remain in an upright and locked position much longer.

"The strategy of rapid growth was incompatible with the systems for managing the work force," asserts Pfeffer. "For instance, rapid growth is incompatible with a 1:100 employee selection ratio and with extensive cross-training—and led ultimately to the organization's demise."

People's Express went bankrupt in 1986. Texas Air eventually purchased what was left of the once high-flying airline.

{
BUSINESS MORAL:
*Make sure your planning, processes,
and systems are compatible with your
overall business strategy.*
}

SOURCE

Pfeffer, Jeffrey. *Competitive Advantage Through People: Unleashing the Power of the Work Force,* 228–29. Boston, MA: Harvard Business School Press, 1994.

The One-Eyed Doe

A doe had sight in only one eye because of an accident as a fawn. Since she was vulnerable if a predator approached on her blind side, the doe made a habit of grazing on a high cliff overlooking the sea. She kept her good eye landward scouting for predators, and her blind eye toward the ocean.

One day, a boat filled with sailors rowed past the cliff. A sailor spotted the doe, grabbed a bow, and shot her. As the doe lay dying, she gasped, "I assumed my enemies would come by land. I never thought to look out to sea."

{
AESOP'S MORAL:
*Trouble comes from where
we least expect it.*
}

PERSPECTIVE: Every business strategy contains assumptions about what will happen in the future, but nobody has a crystal ball and nothing is certain. The economy rises and falls, employees come and go, government enacts new laws and repeals old ones, new products and technologies blossom and fade, and people's tastes change. The best that you can do as a businessperson is to collect as much information as possible, glean trends as best you can, and go forward with plans flexible enough to accommodate significant changes in business conditions.

The downside of having a plan that is based on faulty assumptions or is too inflexible to change can be enormous. Look at what happened to AT&T when it launched an ill-conceived and inflexible plan for growth, as described in *Execution: The Discipline of Getting Things Done* by Larry Bossidy and Ram Charan.

Michael Armstrong became CEO of AT&T in 1997. At that time, the company's profits came primarily from long-distance calls and data transfer. But the business was changing, and long-distance telephone rates were falling as new companies entered the market. Armstrong shaped a strategy to get AT&T into new growth markets. His plan had four components: (1) buy cable companies to get direct access to customers; (2) bundle services so that customers could obtain more communication options through one company; (3) execute these changes fast enough to offset declining long-distance revenues; and (4) assume the 1996 Telecommunications Act would buy AT&T some time by precluding local telecommunications companies from competing in long distance.

The strategy looked brilliant at face value—but ended up being a complete failure. What happened? Bossidy and Charan explain: "For the strategy to succeed, all four of the building blocks had to be sound. But all turned out to be based on faulty assumptions. The cable acquisitions were costly: AT&T paid top dollar for them and then some. At the same time, long distance prices declined faster than assumed. Consumers weren't as interested in bundled services as AT&T had expected . . . Finally, the regulators did not enforce the Telecommunications Act as well as AT&T had hoped."

This last development was doubly critical: local companies swarmed into the long-distance market, and long-distance carriers had a lot less local access than they had planned on. "AT&T's strategy was disconnected from both external and internal realities,"

Bossidy and Charan conclude. "It didn't test its critical assumptions to see if they were robust, and it had no alternative plan for what to do if one or more of them proved wrong."

{
BUSINESS MORAL:
Test critical assumptions to make sure they're grounded in reality.
}

SOURCE

Bossidy, Larry, and Ram Charan. *Execution: The Discipline of Getting Things Done,* 179–81. New York: Crown Business, 2002.

The Donkey, the Rooster, *and* the Lion

A donkey and a rooster were barnyard friends. One day a hungry lion lurking nearby saw the donkey and decided to eat him for breakfast. Now, legend has it that nothing irritates a lion as much as the sound of a rooster crowing. When the rooster saw the lion ready to pounce on his friend, he let out an especially loud cock-a-doodle-do. Greatly vexed by the noise, the lion turned tail and raced into the woods.

"That's right. You'd better run!" the donkey shouted.

Thrilled that he and his friend had bested the king of beasts, the foolish donkey galloped after the lion to rout him further. But as soon as the lion was out of earshot of the rooster, he spun around to face his long-eared pursuer.

"Isn't that funny? I can't hear that annoying rooster anymore," the drooling lion said to the startled, wide-eyed donkey. "So it looks like I can eat my breakfast in peace!"

With that, the lion pounced and devoured the donkey on the spot.

{
AESOP'S MORAL:
False confidence is the precursor of disaster.
}

PERSPECTIVE: Whether it was false confidence or simple arrogance, the donkey's ill-advised pursuit ended in disaster. Better for the animal if he had enjoyed his victory and left well enough alone instead of violating the forty-seventh law of power, based on Robert Greene and Joost Elffers's book, *The 48 Laws of Power*. Law Number 47 states, "Do not go past the mark you aimed for; in victory, learn when to stop. In the heat of victory, arrogance and overconfidence can push you past the goal you had aimed for, and by going too far, you make more enemies than you defeat. Do not allow success to go to your head. There is no substitute for strategy and careful planning. Set a goal and when you reach it, stop."

Greene and Elffers cite the cautionary tale of Cyrus the Great (circa 600–529 BC), king of Persia. Cyrus was a skillful warrior who led a successful rebellion against the Medes and their king. In 546 BC, he added the kingdom of Lydia to the Persian Empire. In 539 BC, he overran and captured the kingdom of Babylon. Cyrus was a merciful ruler who allowed the Israelites to return to Israel from their exile in Babylon and rebuild the temple of Solomon. Only when Cyrus violated the forty-seventh law of power did he realize his ruin.

Cyrus decided to attack an eastern tribe called the Massagetae, led by their queen, Tomyris. As a trick, Cyrus posted a small guard on the queen's side of the river, commanding his men to watch over a lavish banquet until he and the rest of his troops got there. But before Cyrus arrived, a division of the queen's army, commanded by her son, attacked the guard and easily defeated it. Just as Cyrus had hoped, the victors sat down and gorged themselves on the food and wine rather than let all of it go to waste.

When Cyrus counterattacked soon afterward, the Massagetae were too drunk to defend themselves. The Persians easily defeated them and captured the queen's son in the process—a major victory for Cyrus.

Queen Tomyris sent a messenger asking for peace and the safe return of her son. Cyrus refused; he wanted an even greater victory.

As both sides prepared for war, the queen subsequently learned that her son had committed suicide; his shame at being captured was too much for him to bear.

The aggrieved woman called in every favor owed her, summoned all of her allies, attacked the Persians with superior numbers, and soundly defeated them. Her soldiers captured and decapitated Cyrus. The queen then placed his head in a wine cask filled with blood.

The Persian Empire quickly fell apart without Cyrus as a unifying force. All of his prior good works and sociological advances went for naught because of his one brash act. As the ancient Japanese proverb cautions: "When you have won a great victory, tighten the strings of your helmet."

{ **BUSINESS MORAL:**
*The moment of victory is often
the moment of greatest peril.* }

SOURCE

Greene, Robert, and Joost Elffers. *The 48 Laws of Power,* 410–12. New York: Viking, 1998.

Human Resources

(Conflict Resolution)

Strike a balance between confidence and humility—enough confidence to know that you can make a real difference, enough humility to ask for help.

—CARLY FIORINA
(CEO OF HEWLETT-PACKARD, 1954–)

It is virtue not to be vicious.

—AESOP

The Wolf *and* the Lamb

A wolf stopped to drink from a brook and saw a lamb just downstream. The wolf began to drool.

I'll need to come up with a good reason to gobble up this innocent creature that's done me no harm, he thought.

The wolf shouted over to the lamb: "How dare you muddy the water while I'm trying to get a drink!"

The lamb meekly replied, "How can that be? I'm downstream of you."

"Are you calling me a liar?" the wolf snarled. "In fact, I think someone told me you were spreading lies about me last year."

The lamb began to shake and said, "That couldn't be, because I wasn't even born a year ago."

"Then it must have been your father, which amounts to the same insult," the wolf growled as he pounced on the lamb and ate him.

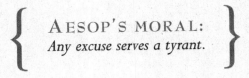

AESOP'S MORAL:
Any excuse serves a tyrant.

PERSPECTIVE: Ever had a boss like the wolf? "There is probably nothing worse in business than to work for a boss that doesn't want you to win," says General Electric's Jack Welch. Nothing is ever good enough, accurate enough, timely enough, or thorough enough for this type of person. A boss may not want you to succeed for several reasons: he's insecure, she views you as a threat, or he doesn't like your "type." The reasons are not as important as the repercussions. When the boss has it in for you, and it's clear that he intends to eat you for lunch, then it's time for a change. Unfortunately, most people find change hard and try to stick it out. Lee Iacocca has one word of advice for those trying to ride out a bad situation: *don't*. In his autobiography, he explains what happened when his boss turned on him.

Iacocca was president of the Ford Motor Company in 1975. His track record in designing and producing automobiles was stellar and showed a long string of successes, including his pet project, the Mustang, a car that made automobile history and put him on the covers of both *Time* and *Newsweek*. Everything was going Iacocca's way until he learned that his boss, Henry Ford II, grandson of the legend, wanted him out of the company.

Why did Ford want Iacocca out? To this day, people aren't sure. Some believe that Ford didn't want someone from outside the Ford family running the company. Others think that Ford didn't want an Italian running the company. Iacocca believes that Ford perceived him as a threat. Whatever the reason, Ford turned into a wolf searching for any justification to get rid of his second in command.

Ford shelled out more than $2 million on private investigators to come up with dirt on Iacocca. As hard as they tried, the spies turned up nothing. Next, Ford asked senior executives to help him compile a list of Iacocca's friends at Ford. List in hand, Ford fired each person in turn. Iacocca realized his work situation was quickly deteriorating as he watched his friends walk out the door one by one. Finally, Ford hired a management consultant to reorganize the company. When the smoke cleared, Ford demoted Iacocca from the number two person in the organization to number three. How much more abuse and intimidation could Iacocca withstand?

"I often ask myself why I didn't quit at the end of 1975," Iacocca said. "Why did I accept the fate Henry was dishing out? First, like anybody who's in a bad situation, I hoped that things would get better. Maybe Henry would come to his senses. Or the board would get its back up. Why did I stay? In part because I couldn't imagine working anywhere else. I had spent my whole adult life at Ford, and that's where I wanted to be. Deep down in my character there must have been a weakness."

When Ford realized that he couldn't bully Iacocca into quitting, he fired him. Chrysler Corporation, in financial trouble at the time, immediately hired Iacocca, who helped turn the company around with his new pet project: the minivan.

Bully bosses come in various forms according to Workplace Bullying & Trauma Institute, an advocacy group based in Bellingham, Washington, as described in a recent *New York Times* article. The *snake*, the most common bully, smiles to your face and then backstabs you as soon as you leave the room. The *screamer* loves to display his temper publicly. The *nitpicker* criticizes constantly in the hope of undermining your confidence. The *gatekeeper* is distant, cold, and calculating. She plays favorites. If she likes you, you'll succeed. If she doesn't, you can expect a work life filled with resentment and frustration.

Iacocca's situation was unique; because he was the number two person in the organization, he had no one above him to help him out with Ford. If you're having trouble with your boss, it's sometimes possible to go above your boss's head to plead your case. But be careful: it's a risky move that could backfire if your boss finds out, and you'll end up making your job situation even worse. Absent an intervening angel from higher up in the organization, though, you're stuck. You can sit and wait and hope the situation improves, which is most people's first impulse, or you can make the first move and request a transfer or get another job before the ax falls.

{ BUSINESS MORAL:
Don't sit back and do nothing when the boss has it in for you. }

SOURCES

Carey, Benedict. "Fear in the Workplace: The Bullying Boss." *New York Times*, June 22, 2004, D6.

Iacocca, Lee. *Iacocca: An Autobiography,* 116–21. New York: Bantam Books, 1984.

Welch, Jack. *Jack: Straight from the Gut,* 66. New York: Warner Books, 2001.

Jupiter, Neptune, Minerva, *and* Momus

Back in the days when the world was new, Jupiter, Neptune, and Minerva had great arguments about which god could make the most perfect object. The three decided to have a contest to see which of their creations came closest to perfection. They asked the god Momus to be the arbiter.

Jupiter made a man; Neptune, a bull; and Minerva, a house. Momus studied the three creations.

He immediately found fault with Jupiter's man: "There's no window in his breast so that we can see his innermost feelings and desires."

Next, he took issue with the bull. "Its horns are above its eyes. How can the animal see when it gores with them?" Momus said disdainfully.

Finally, Momus pointed to a flaw of the house. "It has no wheels to let the owners move away from noisy neighbors," he said.

Jupiter became irate at the god who criticized everything, and drove him from Olympus.

{
AESOP'S MORAL:
Those who produce the least are the ones who criticize the most.
}

PERSPECTIVE: Imagine having a boss like Momus. You'd go to work each day assured that nothing you did would ever be good enough.

You might even develop an inferiority complex and start questioning your abilities, which is exactly how overly critical supervisors want you to feel. In *Ground Rules for Winners*, Joe Torre, former manager of the Atlanta Braves, describes how he confronted an overly critical boss named Ted ("If I only had a little humility, I'd be perfect") Turner.

Turner hired Torre to run his baseball team in 1982. Torre worked out a three-year contract with Atlanta's general manager, John Mullen. The contract included an attendance clause awarding Torre a bonus if more than two million people came to the ballpark in any given year. Things quickly got off to a bad start. Mullen let Torre know that he wasn't his first choice to manage the team. Next, Torre found out that Mullen had never informed Turner about the attendance clause. Turner, who made it a point to avoid such clauses, struck it from the contract. Things went downhill from there.

The Braves were losing so badly by the middle innings of one game that Torre decided to pinch-hit some of his younger players. He reasoned that he'd save his veterans in case the game got close in the later innings. The press slammed Torre the next day for keeping the veterans on the bench. Later that afternoon, Turner asked for a meeting with Torre. Turner agreed with the press that Torre blew the game and made his point by screaming at Torre in front of a group of people from the Braves' front office. Torre was incensed, but waited until after the ball game, which the Braves won, before he asked to see Turner privately.

Torre confronted Turner: "Ted, you're the owner and I respect you because of that. You can fire me or make any changes you want. But don't you ever yell at me like that in front of other people. If you scream at me, fine. Just do it in private."

Turner listened but never apologized, and the two men never developed a mutual trust. Eventually, Turner fired Torre.

"You can't always thrive in an organization," Torre says. "But you can always hold on to your integrity. In fact, when you survive a bad work situation with your integrity intact, you may even feel better about yourself."

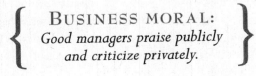

{
BUSINESS MORAL:
*Good managers praise publicly
and criticize privately.*
}

SOURCE

Torre, Joe. *Joe Torre's Ground Rules for Winners: 12 Keys to Managing Team Players, Tough Bosses, Setbacks and Success,* 204–7. New York: Hyperion, 1999.

The Mischievous Dog

A man owned an unruly dog that just wouldn't behave. The animal refused to be trained. One day the dog bit the man as he was trying to play with him.

"That's it," the master said in a fit of exasperation. "I'm getting rid of you once and for all."

As the man dragged the dog into the woods, a neighbor came up to him and offered a suggestion.

"The way to tame that unruly beast is to fasten a heavy chain around his neck. That will stop him from biting, and it will be proof to everybody not to go near the animal."

The man liked the suggestion and chained the beast. The dog looked down at his chain and thought it a badge of distinction. When the man and the dog went to the marketplace, the dog purposefully rattled the chain to get everyone's attention.

An old dog limped over to the unruly animal and said, "I wouldn't make so much noise if I were you. Wearing a chain like that is no honor. It more likely confirms what an incorrigible beast you really are."

{ **AESOP'S MORAL:**
People often mistake notoriety for fame. }

PERSPECTIVE: Have you ever had a "dog" of an employee working for you whose performance was chronically subpar? How did you handle the situation? How did you decide between keeping and firing the employee? Most companies go out of their way to keep employees, preferring to issue them warnings, put them on probation, and counsel or retrain them rather than let them go. After all, good help is hard to find.

Whether you are going to keep or dismiss a marginal employee, though, your first step is the same: *document the problem*. The chain around the neck of the mischievous dog was the first documentation that the animal's behavior was a problem. Nobody likes to sit down with a worker and discuss poor job performance, but it's essential to let workers know where they stand, including the problem, the solution, and the schedule for turning around performance.

Workers are more likely to accept criticism and modify behavior if you present specific examples of nonperformance or how performance could be improved. Try not to use general statements such as, "You're not a team player," or "You're not pulling your weight." Instead, provide specific documentation: "During January's inventory count, you completed only half the audits that your counterparts did according to these records. Many of them complained you were dogging it."

Do your best to help an employee turn bad performance into good, but don't be afraid to face the business reality that some people just don't belong on the payroll. Nobody likes firing an employee, but everybody recognizes it as a fact of life. I'll never forget the first time I had to dismiss one of our engineers. It was a painful but instructive experience.

Don came to my team through our Employee Rotation Program. All new hires had the chance to spend the first two years of their careers working in six-month stints in different parts of the company. The idea was to expose them to various types of work with the hope that, after two years, they would find a nice fit for themselves doing something they liked.

Don was starting his third six-month tour of duty. My team started complaining about him two days after his arrival. I investigated the complaints and found all of them justified. He came to work late, left early, did sloppy work when he wasn't talking to his friends on the phone, and was unable to complete rudimentary tasks. The guy looked to be bad news. I wondered if he had problems in his two previous assignments, so I went to Human Resources and pulled his file. His first supervisor never filled out a performance review. His second supervisor had filled one out and rated him as "meeting expectations." Clearly, something was amiss.

I visited both of Don's previous supervisors and asked them what they thought of his performance when he worked for them. "I never filled out a performance review for the guy because it would have been awful," the first supervisor said. "I couldn't think of anything good to say, and if I wrote down what I truly felt, his career here would have been over before it started."

Don's second supervisor confirmed my worst fears: "He was a terrible employee and nothing but trouble from the moment he got here. He never seemed to grasp the work assignments, and anything he did, I had to do over."

"Then *why* did you rate him as meeting expectations?" I asked through slightly clenched teeth.

"I knew he'd rotate out of my group in a few months and he wouldn't be my problem anymore," he replied honestly.

The failure of these two supervisors to address the problem wasn't fair to me, it wasn't fair to the company, and most important, it wasn't fair to Don. It fell to me to correct the situation. I decided to give him a chance to improve his performance. If he improved, he could stay. If he didn't, I would dismiss him.

First, I went to HR and asked for advice. "Document the problem," they said. "Right now, the only paperwork on Don has him meeting expectations, and if he doesn't turn things around, you have absolutely no grounds to dismiss him."

I filled out a performance review form and rated him as "failing to meet expectations." I met with Don, discussed the form, gave him specific instances of where his performance was unacceptable, and told him what he needed to do to improve. I gave him one month to turn things around.

He didn't. In fact, his performance got worse. Clearly, Don had to go, but at least I had the documentation I needed to dismiss him. When the day came, I went to his cubicle and found him sound asleep with his head on his desk. Firing him became easier by the minute. I brought him into my office where a rep from HR was already seated, closed the door, and gave him the bad news.

Do you know what his reaction was? He let out a huge sigh and said, "Thank goodness, it's over." He explained that he really didn't belong at the company, felt intimidated by all the smart people around him, and didn't like the work. He actually thanked me for letting him go because he could pursue the kind of work he wanted to do. I never asked him what kind of work that was. To this day, I've always wondered. I pray it wasn't medicine.

It took a lot more time and energy for our company to deal with Don because we let the problem fester. Nevertheless, we learned a valuable lesson about how to address bad performance directly. During your career, you may run into other reasons for having to dismiss an employee. According to *The Termination Handbook* by Robert

Coulson, the most common reasons for dismissal are poor job performance, absenteeism, alcoholism, on-the-job drug use, fighting, violation of plant rules, unprovoked insubordination, dishonesty, and sexual harassment.

Whatever the reason, dismissing someone is never pleasant or easy. But if you have no other choice, do it the right way by following the four steps recommended by Daniel Kingsley in *How to Fire an Employee*:

1. *Document the problem*. We learned this lesson the hard way. Documentation protects you against lawsuits claiming unjust termination or discrimination, and refutes any claims that the employee wasn't warned that he was "at risk." If the employee is being dismissed as part of a general layoff, specify why the workforce is being reduced.

2. *Plan the dismissal*. Decide who will do the terminating and who will act as a third party and witness. Coordinate the reason for the dismissal, and develop a suitable cover story that is agreeable to the employee and to management.

3. *Schedule the day and time*. Schedule the termination in the morning and on any day *except* Friday. "It's depressing for an employee to have to go home on a Friday without a job," Kingsley quotes one business executive. "Early in the week a person has more strength to take that kind of thing."

4. *Conduct a dress rehearsal*. Leave nothing to chance. Draft a one-sided dialogue, and read from it if necessary during the actual termination.

I'd add a fifth and final recommendation:

5. *Keep it short.* Don't protract the agony on dismissal day. The longer the dismissal session goes, the greater the chance for the employee to become upset. Remain calm at all times.

Remember: hiring and firing are different sides of the same coin. So if you hire well, you'll spend less time having to fire well.

> **BUSINESS MORAL:**
> *One of the more difficult decisions a company must make is whether to keep or dismiss a nonperforming worker.*

SOURCES

Coulson, Robert. *The Termination Handbook,* 84–85. New York: Free Press, 1981.

Kingsley, Daniel. *How to Fire an Employee: An Essential Guide to Humane, Fair, and Effective Techniques for All Responsible Business People,* 58, 158–59, 166–67, 170. New York: Facts on File, 1984.

Human Resources

(Motivating and Inspiring)

God didn't have time to create a nobody—just a somebody. I believe that each of us has God-given talents within us waiting to be brought into fruition. Every person is unique and special.

—MARY KAY ASH
(FOUNDER, MARY KAY COSMETICS, 1918–2001)

Do all the good you can to all people . . . and do no hurt however, where you can do no good.

—AESOP

The Fox *and* the Crow

A crow swooped down and stole a piece of cheese from a table and then soared to the top of a tall tree to enjoy the morsel. A fox saw the crow with the cheese and thought: *I think I know a way to get that cheese.*

Standing at the bottom of the tree, the fox yelled up to the crow: "Good day, Sister Crow. You look well today. Your wings are glossy, your feathers are as smooth as an eagle's, and your claws look as sharp as razors. I didn't hear you sing yet, but I bet your voice is as sweet as any bird's in the forest."

The crow, believing every word the fox said, loved the flattery. Other animals complained that her caw grated on their ears. She decided to prove to the fox how right he was. But as she opened her beak to sing, the cheese fell out. The fox snagged it in midair and gobbled it up.

As he walked away, the fox said, "You might want to remain silent the next time someone praises you."

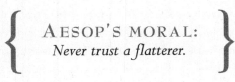

AESOP'S MORAL:
Never trust a flatterer.

PERSPECTIVE: The American philosopher John Dewey said that the deepest urge in human nature is "the desire to be important." That urge manifests itself at your office in the desire to be appreciated.

131

Your people want to be complimented on their talents and to know you value the work they do. It's true for everyone who works for you and with you: the scientist, the waitress, the office boy, or the person who answers your phones. All want to feel that they *matter*. But showing them that you appreciate their individual contributions takes thought and effort. It's too easy to come across as a mere flatterer.

What's the difference between appreciation and flattery? "That is simple," says Dale Carnegie in *How to Win Friends and Influence People*. "One is sincere and the other insincere. One comes from the heart out; the other from the teeth out. One is unselfish; the other selfish. One is universally admired; the other universally condemned."

I'm sure you've heard of the saying: "Flattery will get you everywhere." Don't believe it. Workers gradually learn to ignore empty flattery and mistrust flatterers. In the long run, flattery won't work with discerning people. But true, heartfelt appreciation can actually make a difference in a person's life. Dale Carnegie goes on to tell the story he first heard on one of Paul Harvey's radio broadcasts, *The Rest of the Story*.

Many years ago, a mouse scampered across the floor of a Detroit classroom and then disappeared. The teacher, Mrs. Beneduci, asked one of her students, Stevie Morse, to help her find it, even though he was blind. The teacher valued the child's special ability to acutely hear things, which compensated for his lack of eyesight. It was one of the first times somebody appreciated the boy's keen sense of hearing.

The children became as silent as snowflakes as Stevie listened for the mouse. The little boy pointed in the direction of a wastebasket. Sure enough, Mrs. Beneduci found the little critter hiding behind it. Years later, Stevie Morse would change his name to Little Stevie Wonder and would reference his teacher's act of appreciation as a turning point in his life. Stevie Wonder has earned seventeen Grammy Awards and an

Oscar. He has sold more than seventy million LPs and ranks alongside the Beatles and Elvis Presley in having the most Top Ten records.

A final thought: to appreciate your workers, you must know them personally. Only after you've invested your time and effort to know your workers as individuals, understand how well they do their jobs, and how they contribute to your company's success, can you meaningfully appreciate them and give them the kind of validation they seek and deserve. Otherwise, your attempts to praise will come across as empty as the conniving crow's.

> { **BUSINESS MORAL:**
> *The best managers genuinely
> appreciate their employees.* }

SOURCES

Aurandt, Paul. *Paul Harvey's The Rest of the Story,* 29–31. Edited and compiled by Lynne Harvey. Garden City, NY: Doubleday, 1977.

Carnegie, Dale. *How to Win Friends and Influence People,* 47, 56–58. New York: Simon and Schuster, 1964.

The Gnat *and* the Bull

A bull was lolling about in a big meadow. A gnat came buzzing around and eventually settled on one of the bull's horns.

"Friend Bull, I hope I'm not inconveniencing you in any way," the insect said. "If my added weight is too much for you, please let me know and I'll fly off."

The bull smiled and said, "Don't worry about your extra weight, my arrogant little friend. Truth be told, I wasn't even aware you were there!"

{
AESOP'S MORAL:
Sometimes the smaller the mind, the bigger the ego.
}

PERSPECTIVE: What qualities do you seek in new job candidates? If you're like most people, you *expect* punctuality and a nice appearance. But how do you decide among various candidates whose experience and salary requirements are about equal? How often is a hiring approach a process of elimination? What qualities have job candidates displayed that turned you off? Would you consider hiring a candidate who came across as self-aggrandizing as the gnat? What kind of attitude does your company like to see?

People with bad attitudes can harm a business in many ways: creating morale problems, wanting too much too soon, refusing to learn new skills, or working as loners instead of as members of a team. People with bad attitudes can be arrogant, mean-spirited, overcontrolling, or insecure. That's why it's essential to do the best job possible when hiring. How important is the right attitude when screening prospective employees? At Southwest Airlines, it's everything, according to Joan Magretta in *What Management Is*.

Southwest has been the biggest airline success story for more than thirty years. The recipe for Southwest's success includes its focused, no-frills, point-to-point travel routes as well as its motivated and productive workforce. Even though Southwest is heavily unionized, it has avoided implementing constricting work rules. This allows each employee to pitch in and undertake whatever tasks need to be done. The airline has shortened gate turnaround times: a Southwest crew of six can do in fifteen minutes what other airlines require a twelve-person crew and thirty-five minutes to do.

Southwest recognizes that people are its cornerstone. Consequently, the company goes out of its way to hire the best employees. "Hire for attitude, train for skill" is one of Southwest's mottoes. According to Magretta, Southwest screens about 200,000 applicants a year, interviews 35,000, and hires 4,000. In 2003, the company screened 202,357 applicants and hired 908 of them.

What's the airline looking for? Southwest's founding CEO, Herb Kelleher, is clear on that point: "We draft great attitudes. If you don't have a good attitude, we don't want you, no matter how skilled you are. We can change skill levels through training. We can't change attitude." Peers, not a Human Resources Department, screen job applicants. Pilots interview pilots, and baggage handlers interview baggage handlers. And the common denominator that unites all new hires is their great attitude.

So far, so good. But what constitutes a great attitude? Each of us may define a great attitude differently, but we may generally include these common attributes: someone who is enthusiastic, enjoys working with people, likes to learn new things, demonstrates initiative, has a good sense of humor, willingly accepts responsibility, is eager to help, and shows confidence without being obnoxious, unlike the gnat in the fable.

How can you determine whether a person has a great attitude? Ask some pointed questions during the interview. Robert Half, author of *On Hiring*, provides questions that can help you identify candidates with the right attitude:

Could you tell me why you're interested in this job? Weed out the candidates who are looking for any kind of job from the ones who are genuinely interested in and enthusiastic about your company.

Why have you decided to leave your present position? This question can help you nail down what motivates a candidate.

What would you like to be earning two years from now? Does this person have a realistic sense of his worth in the industry? Or is the person's ego so big you can see trouble ahead?

What do you consider your most significant accomplishments in your business life? Look for pride and enthusiasm.

What have been some failures or frustrations in your business life? How comfortable is he admitting weaknesses? Can he laugh at himself?

What risks did you take in your last few jobs, and what was the result? This question can separate outstanding candidates from ho-hum applicants. People who are willing to take risks are also more likely to be willing to learn new skills and take on challenging assignments.

Think about something you consider a failure in your life, and tell me why you think it occurred. Does the candidate accept responsibility or blame others?

How did you enjoy working for your former employer? Is the candidate a complainer with a track record of not getting along with others? Excessive criticism of a former employer might be a warning sign.

What do you do when you're having trouble solving a problem? Is the candidate independent? Resourceful? Willing to tap into others?

What did you do in your last job to make yourself more effective? Is the candidate eager to learn or willing to try new things?

What are your hobbies and interests? A candidate's outside interests can sometimes give you a better picture of who he is as a person.

Describe the best boss you ever had. This question can help you figure out what kind of supervision the candidate needs or whether the candidate accepts criticism graciously.

What's the most monotonous job you ever had? A candidate who has successfully performed in a job with a lot of monotony (and let's face it, every job has *some* monotony) shows an ability to cope.

{
BUSINESS MORAL:
The best new hire is the one with the right experience at the right salary and the right attitude.
}

SOURCES

Half, Robert. *On Hiring*, 119-25. New York: Crown Publishers, 1985.

Magretta, Joan. *What Management Is, How It Works, and Why It's Everyone's Business*, 207–8. New York: Free Press, 2002.

The Hare *and* the Tortoise

A hare enjoyed making fun of a tortoise's slowness. "You're so slow," the hare liked to say, "that sheep count *you* before they go to sleep!"

Usually, the tortoise quietly endured the taunts, but one day he lost his patience in front of the other animals.

"Since you think you're so fast, I challenge you to a race," the tortoise said.

The hare was incredulous: "You can't be serious! There's no way a pokey creature like you could beat me."

"Then you accept my challenge!" the tortoise confirmed loudly so all the other creatures could hear.

The day of the race came. The animals set the course and selected the fox as judge. The hare and the tortoise crouched at the starting line. The fox yelled, "Go!" and the race was on.

The hare shot ahead of the tortoise in a cloud of dust and quickly became a dot on the horizon, while the tortoise lumbered along. The hare raced so far ahead of the tortoise that he decided to sit down and rest. The warm sun made him drowsy.

I'm so far ahead, the hare thought to himself, *that I have time to take a quick nap before I finish the race.*

Meanwhile, the tortoise never lost his confidence or his resolve. He crept along until he passed the dozing hare and ambled toward the finish line as the rest of the animals cheered him on. The shouts woke the hare, who looked up to see the tortoise inching toward victory. The hare ran as fast as he could, but he was just too far behind to catch up. The tortoise crossed the finish line and won the race to the other animals' delight. The greatly-humiliated hare retreated to the woods.

{ AESOP'S MORAL:
Slow and steady wins the race. }

PERSPECTIVE: The tortoise was confident in who he was, what he could do, and what he couldn't do. He believed his perseverance and resolve could outlast the formidable fleetness of his furry competitor, and he was right, enabling him to prevail against overwhelming odds.

No two employees are alike; every employee has special talents and gifts. Some employees are fast starters; others are late bloomers. One of your objectives as a manager should be to draw out the special talents of each employee to serve the best interests of the company. What's the best way to do that? Rick Pitino believes he has the answer.

Pitino has coached basketball at the college and professional levels. He led the Kentucky Wildcats to the NCAA championship in 1996. In *Success Is a Choice,* Pitino describes how he helped professional basketball player and late bloomer Mark Jackson realize his unique talents.

Jackson was the eighteenth pick of the first round of the National Basketball Association in 1987 when Pitino was head coach of the New York Knicks. Jackson was an outstanding guard at St. John's, but the fact that seventeen teams passed on him raised concerns about his future as a professional. The line on Jackson was that he was too slow, couldn't shoot very well, and would have trouble keeping up with quicker guards in the league. From the beginning,

Pitino was determined to raise Jackson's confidence and self-esteem, especially as his top draft pick went through a period of self-doubt. Jackson believed he was destined to fail, fueled in part by what he read in the New York tabloids. "Too slow for the amount of money he's being paid," they said.

Pitino explains: "One of the first things I did was tell the rest of the team I thought Mark had a legitimate chance to be Rookie of the Year because he would flourish in our system." Understandably, the rest of the team did not believe Pitino. An eighteenth-round draft pick doesn't go on to become Rookie of the Year. Pitino focused on accentuating Jackson's strengths—his passing, his ability to lead, and his personal charisma. He dispelled Jackson's self-doubt about his slowness by telling him that there was no other point guard in the league he wanted more on his team, except for Magic Johnson. Jackson's self-esteem and confidence grew daily. And so did his level of play.

The next spring, Mark Jackson was selected as the NBA's Rookie of the Year. No other player before or since has been picked as low in the draft as Jackson and gone on to win Rookie of the Year. "You can expect great things from people," Pitino says, "who feel good about themselves."

{ **BUSINESS MORAL:** *Help workers gain confidence by building on their strengths.* }

SOURCE

Pitino, Rick. *Success Is a Choice: Ten Steps to Overachieving in Business and Life,* 13–15. New York: Broadway Books, 1997.

The Peasant *and* the Apple Tree

————

A small apple tree growing in the middle of a peasant's garden never blossomed. Each year, the peasant grew increasingly frustrated at the tree's barrenness, and one day he decided to cut it down.

The sparrows and crickets who made their nests in its branches begged the peasant not to do it.

"This tree is valuable," they said. "Destroy it and you will force us to find new homes elsewhere. You won't hear our singing and chirping anymore."

The peasant ignored their pleas, grabbed his ax, and began hacking away. But after several strokes, he realized the tree was hollow. More curiously, the tree was dripping a yellow liquid. The peasant looked inside the trunk and found a hive of bees making a large store of honey.

Delighted with his discovery, the peasant thought to himself: *Why, this small tree is more valuable than I realized and worth keeping after all!*

{
AESOP'S MORAL:
True value is sometimes hidden.
}

PERSPECTIVE: Which of your talents helped you get where you are today? When did you realize you had those talents? Were you always aware of them, or did you discover them over time? Did somebody ever help you uncover a hidden talent? How did that person do it? Did you ever benefit from somebody giving you a big break so you could use those talents? How do you think your life would have changed if you hadn't received that break?

Each of us quietly holds untapped potential, and sometimes all it takes to unleash that potential is a new opportunity to show what we can do. "Small opportunities," Demosthenes wrote, "are often the beginning of great enterprises."

I remember my first big opportunity to prove myself, my first big break. I was a low-level engineer working on a million-dollar project to protect drinking water supplies in southern New Jersey. Things weren't going well. First, the project manager and the client clashed, forcing the company to assign a new project manager. Soon afterward, the replacement manager decided to leave the company for another job. The project was a mess: the client was angry, the budget was just about gone, and the work wasn't finished. One of the division heads approached me about taking over the job and stabilizing the situation. Some of my peers warned of an impending *Titanic*-like disaster. They thought I was crazy when I said yes. I figured it was my first chance to be captain, to be in charge, to call the shots, even though there was the nagging possibility that I might go down with the ship.

Over the next six months, I flew to the Garden State every week to work with the client to understand exactly what he needed and wanted, which turned out to be my first one-on-one interaction with a client. To control costs, I cut the number of people working on the job to a talented few. And I wrote many sections of the final report on my own time because it was clear the client was not about to give us more money to finish the work.

The situation turned around. The client loved the report. We kept the cost overrun to a minimum. More important, I developed a reputation as someone who could put out fires, restore damaged business relationships, and manage bigger contracts. By offering me this opportunity, my supervisor helped me unlock my potential and get my career off and running.

Of course, a great deal of motivation is needed to accept a new opportunity. "Opportunities and motivation are connected," says author and leadership expert John Maxwell. "Motivated people see opportunities, and opportunities are often what motivate people." Consider the Cinderella story of Susan Diaz, as related by Gloria and Thomas Mayer in *Goldilocks on Management*.

Susan, a forty-seven-year-old woman with two college degrees, decided to reenter the workforce after staying at home for seventeen years to raise her children. During that time, she worked hard both inside and outside her home, serving as president of the PTA for six years, and fund-raising on behalf of several worthy causes. Although out of the workforce for almost two decades, Susan got an entry-level job as a secretary in a law firm at $12.50 an hour.

She reported directly to Evelyn Naughton, a partner in the firm. Months passed. Evelyn was cordial to Susan but never really got to know her and what she could do. One of Susan's responsibilities was to attend a planning meeting for an American Cancer Society fund-raiser. No stranger to fund-raising, Susan saw an opportunity to be a big help and volunteered to oversee the entire effort. She worked diligently over the next six months, suggesting creative ways to increase donations.

How did she do? The fund-raiser was a smashing success, bringing in more donations than any in the chapter's history. But her story doesn't end there. While working on the project, Susan met many interesting people, including Ryan Fjelstad, then the CEO of an accounting firm. After watching Susan in action, Ryan quickly realized her enormous potential and offered her a job to run his entire office at an annual salary of $65,000, an offer she greatly appreciated and immediately accepted. Stunned when Susan gave notice, Evelyn was forced to find a replacement for the star that she never realized was sitting next to her.

Opportunities don't always present themselves in the best circumstances. In my case, the opportunity came wrapped in a very unpleasant package. In Susan's case, she took on a big assignment that required a lot of extra time without pay. Sometimes opportunities come in the form of a career setback or demotion. Consider the case of a young African-American woman who became a news anchor only to be subsequently demoted because management didn't think she was right for that kind of job.

The nineteen-year-old became the first African-American to anchor the news at Nashville's WTVF-TV. She did well and, three years later, moved to the bigger Baltimore market to anchor the six o'clock news on WJZ-TV. But her days as a news anchor were numbered. The station's producers concluded that her delivery was just too emotional for hard news stories. They took her off the six o'clock news and relegated her to a morning talk show, *People Are Talking,* to tactfully get rid of her.

Now, most women would have been devastated having a career as a newscaster come to such an abrupt end, but not this woman. What was her reaction? "The minute the first [morning] show was over, I thought, 'Thank God, I've found what I was meant to do. It's like breathing to me.'" The new opportunity that looked like a demotion helped her unlock her potential.

People Are Talking was a big success, beating out the other morning talk show, *Donahue,* in local markets. Seven years later, the woman moved to Chicago to host another talk show, *AM Chicago,* on WLS-TV, where it became the number one talk show in the Windy City. By year's end, the station decided to rename the program *The Oprah Winfrey Show.* "Sometimes you don't choose your career," Oprah says. "It chooses you."

Opportunities can arise out of problems and setbacks. Want a big opportunity? Uncover a big problem and solve it. Opportunities come and go. Be ready. When is the best time to provide an opportunity or, even better, to accept one? How about today?

{
BUSINESS MORAL:
Give employees challenging assignments to help them discover their hidden talents.
}

SOURCES

Lowe, Janet. *Oprah Winfrey Speaks: Insight from the World's Most Influential Voice,* 32–33. New York: John Wiley & Sons, 1998.

Mayer, Gloria Gilbert, and Thomas Mayer. *Goldilocks on Management: 27 Revisionist Fairy Tales for Serious Managers,* 144, 146–48. New York: AMACOM, 1999.

The Goose *and* the Golden Egg

A farmer was amazed one day to find that his goose had laid a solid gold egg. He grabbed the egg and ran to his wife to share the good news. Each day the goose produced a golden egg, and soon the farmer and his wife grew rich. Not satisfied with the production of their prized animal, the two began to brainstorm how they could get even more gold.

"I've got it," the farmer said to his wife. "Let's kill the goose and take the gold out all at once."

His wife agreed. They killed the goose, opened her, and found—nothing.

{ **AESOP'S MORAL:**
Leave well enough alone. }

PERSPECTIVE: How much freedom do you have to call your own shots at work? How much freedom do you give to the people who work for you to call their own shots? Conversely, how often do you check in with your workers to see how they're progressing?

Every one of us wants to feel that the boss cares about what we're doing, but none of us want to get caught up with a control freak who tells us how to do our jobs, continually second-guesses our approach to solving problems, or demands constant progress reports on what we're up to. The amount of freedom we give workers depends directly on how confident we are in the training they received, how much we trust them, and how comfortable we are in delegating work.

Managers meddle for different reasons. Some are insecure about their abilities, so they tend to overmanage. Others are so self-assured, they're adamant that *their* way is the only way to complete a task. But unnecessary intrusions prevent employees from doing their best work.

I once had a two-week deadline to produce a final report on a small research project. I knew what I was doing, but my supervisor felt compelled to get updates from me whenever he had a spare moment, which sometimes turned out to be three or four times *a day*. I appreciated his interest, but his interruptions were definitely counterproductive and bordered on the obsessive. Finally, I had to tell him that if he kept bugging me, I might not make the deadline. I told him that I would send him a brief update via e-mail at the end of each day. He calmed down and stopped interrupting, and I delivered a quality report on time to the client's satisfaction. So what was the problem? It wasn't that my boss didn't trust me—we had worked on similar projects before. I learned that his need to control things grew in inverse proportion to the time available to complete the job: the shorter the deadline, the greater his need to meddle.

Do you recall the film *Butch Cassidy and the Sundance Kid*? Butch (Paul Newman) and Sundance (Robert Redford) go to a Bolivian mine looking for work. The mining boss asks if they can handle a gun because the job requires protecting the company payroll. Throwing a wad of paper down the street, the boss tells Sundance to "hit that." Flat-footed, gun already drawn, arm stiff, the normally dead-aim Sundance shoots but misses the target. As the disappointed boss walks away, Sundance asks, "Can I move?" whereupon he holsters his gun and then rapidly redraws while darting sideways, hitting the target dead on. "I'm better when I move," he says.

Most of us perform better when our supervisors give us room "to move." Our creative ability to develop innovative solutions to problems can burst forth when we are confident in our abilities and know that our supervisors trust us. The more freedom we have to do our jobs, the more empowered we feel, and the better job we do. Want proof? Take a look at how one CEO infused his organization with a no-meddling philosophy to successfully drive innovation.

William McKnight was a pioneer and early innovator at 3M (Minnesota Mining and Manufacturing Company). As president and chairman of the board, he made it a point to publicize his business beliefs throughout the company. "Hire good people and then let them alone to do the job" was one of his core beliefs. McKnight thought that one of management's jobs was to encourage every employee to test new ideas. What was the best way management could accomplish this? Don't meddle. Give each employee space. Let workers experiment because experimentation can lead to innovation. "If you put fences around people," McKnight cautioned, "you get sheep. Give people the room they need."

In *Innovation: Breakthrough Thinking at 3M, DuPont, GE, Pfizer, and Rubbermaid,* 3M's Dr. William E. Coyne describes how the company encourages workers in the research and development division to follow the 15 percent rule: all technical personnel can spend 15 percent of their time working on any project they like. "They need no approvals," Coyne says. "They don't even have to *tell* management what they're working on. No one meters or monitors our people's use of their fifteen percent time."

How important is innovation to 3M? The company invests up to seven cents of every sales dollar into R & D. Innovation involves risk, to be sure, but Coyne believes it's riskier to rely on the familiar.

"Putting bells and whistles on the buggy," he says, "didn't distract consumer attention from the horseless carriage."

Employees of 3M have historically come up with one remarkable product after another, starting back in the 1920s when waterproof sandpaper revolutionized automobile painting. Have you noticed how bright highway signs appear when you drive at night these days? Microreplication technology by 3M created signs that reflect three times more glow from automobile headlights. Other innovative products include new identification cards to prevent counterfeiting and new lightweight and inexpensive lenses for overhead projectors.

Overall, 3M manufactures more than fifty thousand products, including more than nine hundred types of Scotch tape for home, business, and industrial use.

Coyne sums up his boss's philosophy about freedom and innovation: "McKnight decided there was great value in giving innovators creative license, recognizing that sometimes the best thing that management can do is step aside and do nothing."

{
BUSINESS MORAL:
*Hire well, train well, and then
give people the freedom they
need to do their jobs well.*
}

SOURCE

Kanter, Rosabeth Moss, et al. *Innovation: Breakthrough Thinking at 3M, DuPont, GE, Pfizer, and Rubbermaid,* 50–53. New York: HarperBusiness, 1997.

The Ant *and* the Dove

A thirsty ant went to a brook to get a drink. He climbed onto the edge of a blade of grass overhanging the brook, but the surface was so shiny and wet that he lost his balance and fell into the water. A dove sitting in a nearby tree saw the drowning ant and decided to help him.

"I'm going to drop a leaf in the water near you. Climb atop it and save your life," the dove yelled to the ant.

Plucking a leaf from the tree, the dove fluttered just above the ant and then dropped it. The ant scrambled onto the leaf and floated safely to the stream bank.

Just then, a hunter jumped out of the woods with a bow and arrow to shoot the dove. The quick-thinking ant scurried over to the hunter just as he was drawing his bow and bit him on the foot. The hunter yelled in pain, causing him to misfire. The arrow whizzed by the dove, which quickly flew away to safety.

{
AESOP'S MORAL:
One good deed deserves another.
}

PERSPECTIVE: When I was a child, my mother told me to be nice to everybody I met because I would meet some of these same people later in my life. I tried to follow her advice and was amazed at how many times my path did intersect with people I'd met before. As I grew older, I realized that not everybody thought the same way I did. In fact, I worked with some people who were nice only to others they thought could help advance their careers. At company parties, they would ignore anyone lower than they were on the organizational ladder and seek out the big bosses for face time to curry favor. These folks would gush enthusiastically if the CEO was on the elevator in the morning, but couldn't be bothered to give a simple grunt of acknowledgment to the cafeteria worker, secretary, or low-level engineer also on board for the ride.

Most of us aren't cordial and friendly to others because we want something in return. We do it out of simple decency and a desire to connect with other people. That said, being courteous and considerate of others can create interesting fringe benefits, particularly in business. In *Keys to Success,* Napoleon Hill tells of a brief encounter between two people that took an unexpected turn.

An elderly woman walked into a department store in Philadelphia one rainy day. Most of the store's personnel ignored her. But one industrious, respectful clerk approached her and asked her if she wanted any help. The woman replied that she was not interested in buying anything; she merely wanted to wait out the storm in a place where it was dry. The clerk could have ignored her since she wasn't a customer and he wasn't going to sell her any merchandise. Instead, he brought her a chair to make her wait more comfortable.

The rain eventually stopped. As the woman prepared to leave, she asked the considerate clerk for his card. Several months later, the owner of the department store received a letter from the same elderly woman. In the letter she requested that the young clerk who assisted her that rainy afternoon be sent to Scotland to help her furnish an entire castle. The woman turned out to be the mother of billionaire Andrew Carnegie.

Not a bad return for a simple deed performed in kindness, wouldn't you agree? Let me give you another example of how showing a little respect paid back big dividends, in this case, not because of who the woman was, but because of who she would become.

A twenty-year-old woman named Debbi opened a small bakery in Palo Alto, California, in the late 1970s. She contacted local chocolate companies to buy chips for her cookies, which she intended to make her specialty. Her first phone call didn't go well. When the salesman on the other end heard her request for twenty-five pounds of chocolate, he laughed and said, "Listen, sweetheart, when you want ten thousand pounds of chocolate, call me. Otherwise, we're not interested." He hung up on her.

Undaunted, Debbi called a second supplier with the same request. "Where are you located?" he asked. She gave him the address. "I'll be right down," he said.

The man showed up in a car loaded with chocolate chips. She gave him a couple of free cookies and told him what she was trying to do with the business. The man listened attentively and made the young woman feel that she was the only customer he had. He became her chip provider. Within a few years, the young woman's sales exploded. Cookie aficionados everywhere know her by her married name, Mrs. Fields.

What happened to the respectful salesman? "I happen to believe in loyalty and this salesman and his company still have the Mrs. Fields' account today," Debbi said. "We *did* buy more than twenty-five pounds of chocolate from this man. We bought *tons* of chocolate over the next ten years."

{ **BUSINESS MORAL:**
*Treat potential customers
with the same respect as
longtime customers.* }

SOURCES

Fields, Debbi, with Alan Furst. *One Smart Cookie,* 74–75. New York: Simon and Schuster, 1987.

Hill, Napoleon. *Napoleon Hill's Keys to Success: The 17 Principles of Personal Achievement,* 67. New York: Dutton, 1994.

The Donkey *and* the Lapdog

A donkey and a dog lived on the estate of a rich man. The donkey stayed in the stable and had lots of corn and oats to eat. The master used the animal to haul wood and sometimes, at night, to turn the mill. Because he was the master's pet, the dog had it much easier. He got to live in the house and received much of the master's attention.

Look at that mutt, the donkey thought to himself. *He gets to play all day and sit in the master's lap. He does nothing while I'm here breaking my back. Maybe if I started acting like that dog, the master would treat me the same way. I could live in the house, gain more of his affection, and do less work.*

So the next day, the donkey rushed into the house, where the master was eating his lunch, and began frisking about like the dog. The donkey accidentally broke a leg off the table, sending plates and cups crashing to the floor.

"What do you think you're doing, you infernal beast!" the master screamed.

Imitating the dog, the donkey then jumped on the master's lap and pawed him with his hooves.

"Get this creature off me!" the master yelled to his servants. "And put him back where he belongs."

The servants restrained the donkey, took him back to the barn, and weighted him down with so many sticks and stones that the animal couldn't stand up.

{
A ESOP'S MORAL:
*Be content doing what
you're best suited for.*
}

PERSPECTIVE: Companies hate to lose good people. Employee turnover hurts morale, creates inefficiencies, and costs companies money in rehiring and retraining. Worker *dissatisfaction* comes in many flavors: too much work for too little pay, no chance for personal growth or corporate advancement, feeling underappreciated, not feeling like an integral part of the organization, obnoxious coworkers, or incompetent bosses, among others.

Worker *satisfaction*, on the other hand, boils down to one basic issue, and it has nothing to do with salary. It's no secret that workers are happiest and most satisfied when they consider themselves fully engaged in their roles in the company. Do you feel fully engaged at your company? If you're not sure, it might be time for you to conduct a career audit. Here are ten questions to ask:

1. Is the company capitalizing on my special talents?

2. Does my supervisor have my best interests at heart?

3. In the past six months, has my supervisor honestly evaluated my performance?

4. Am I receiving challenging assignments at work to help me grow professionally?

5. Do I have a mentor guiding me as I move up through the organization?

6. Do I have friends at work in whom I can confide?

7. Is there a career track to get me where I want to be in five years?

8. Does my work give me a sense of higher purpose?

9. Are my coworkers trustworthy and committed to excellence?

10. Am I receiving the training I need to do my job well?

A little more praise, recognition, and reassurance by the master of the house would have gone a long way toward engaging the donkey and keeping him happy and content in his work. What's your company's employee turnover rate? How does it compare with that of your competitors? How satisfied are you in your job? What else could your company do to make you feel more engaged?

"The safety of a steady paycheck, a comfortable job that yields decent benefits, and a bearable amount of aggravation can lull you into complacency about your career," says syndicated career columnist Anita Bruzzese. "You may be depriving yourself of challenging, interesting, rewarding work by simply letting your career 'happen.'"

{ BUSINESS MORAL:
*The more you engage your workers,
the less employee turnover you'll have.* }

SOURCE

Bruzzese, Anita. *Take This Job and Thrive: 60 Ways to Make Life More Rewarding in Today's Workplace,* 70. Manassas Park, VA: Impact Publications, 2000.

Marketing Products
and
Services

Anytime you find someone more successful than you are, especially when you are engaged in the same business, you know they are doing something you aren't.

—MALCOLM X
(ACTIVIST, 1925–65)

Watch for opportunities of doing things, for there is nothing well done but what's done in season.

—AESOP

The Two Pots

A flood swept a brass pot and an earthenware pot into a river. The pots were identical in size and shape, and differed only in composition. As they bobbed in the turbulent waters, the brass pot pleaded with its companion to move closer for protection.

"I appreciate your offer to help me," the earthenware pot shouted back, "but I can't afford to get too close to you. If we collide, it'll be the end of me because I'll shatter into a hundred pieces."

{ AESOP'S MORAL:
*Small differences can lead
to big consequences.* }

PERSPECTIVE: How does your product differ from that of your competitors? Is it more user-friendly? Less expensive? Better quality? What kind of packaging do you use?

Companies looking for a competitive edge can sometimes find one just by doing something as simple as changing a product's packaging or its shape. In *The Guerrilla Marketing Handbook,* Jay Levinson and Seth Godin describe how some companies bested the competition with simple innovations in the way they presented their products to customers. Colgate came up with a pump for its toothpaste as an alternative to the squeeze tube. General Electric was one of the first to reduce the amount of packing it put inside its air conditioner boxes, thereby allowing it to reduce the size of the boxes. Even better, GE then put handles on the sides of the boxes, transforming the product from one that required a deliveryman to one that customers could carry out of the store. Chubs turned the packaging for its baby wipes into a product. When the wipes are gone, the package becomes a colorful, stackable LEGO-like toy that kids can play with.

The mail-order rivalry between Montgomery Ward and Sears Roebuck is a classic story of how a small change made a big difference. In 1872 Aaron Montgomery started sending out mail-order catalogs to families in rural areas, primarily farmers. People could buy anything they needed from the catalog: shoes, clothes, furniture, tools, fishing gear. Montgomery's business boomed. Twenty years later, Richard Sears decided to enter the mail-order business. Within eight years, Sears's mail-order business grew bigger than Montgomery's. For the next forty years, Sears dominated all mail-order competition.

What happened? Sears made his catalog smaller and somewhat thinner than Montgomery's catalog. Why smaller? A farmer with several catalogs will naturally stack them on top of one another, placing the smallest on top of the pile. Consequently, the first catalog the farmer reached for when he decided to do his mail ordering was the catalog on top—which always bore the Sears name.

Packaging is everything in the world of cosmetics and perfumes too. Consider how Estee Lauder, a pioneer in the perfume business, packaged one of her most profitable products. In her autobiography, Lauder described developing a new scent during the 1950s called Youth Dew. The first problem she faced was getting American women to buy it since they traditionally didn't buy perfume for themselves. Too self-indulgent! To get over this psychological hurdle, Lauder decided to call her product *bath oil* instead of perfume. She reasoned that a woman wouldn't feel guilty about buying herself a bottle of bath oil.

Lauder's next idea was just as revolutionary. "Why should I make my creation inaccessible? If the bottle were unsealed, a browsing customer could unscrew the cap (as every customer secretly wishes to do), take a whiff, and by the time that occurred, she'd have the essence on her hands. Now, the customer might well leave my counter, but she'd be smelling Youth Dew wherever she went. Chances are that she'd return to the source and buy it for her very own."

The perfume via bath oil was a smash success. Sales soared from $400 a week to $5,000 a week. By 1958, sales had exploded to $800,000 a year. Lauder pioneered other innovations in marketing with her concepts of free samples and "free gift with purchase."

To this day, her company refuses to burden her fragrances with superfluous layers of cellophane or difficult-to-open caps, and her competitors followed her lead. When she died on April 24, 2004, at the age of ninety-seven, she left behind an empire with 21,500 employees and an estimated worth of $10 billion.

{
BUSINESS MORAL:
*Continually look for unique
ways to package your products.*
}

SOURCES

Lauder, Estee. *Estee: A Success Story,* 78–79. New York: Random House, 1985.

Levinson, Jay C., and Seth Godin. *The Guerrilla Marketing Handbook,* 247–50. Boston, MA: Houghton Mifflin, 1994.

Mercury *and* the Sculptor

One day, the fleet-footed god Mercury decided to learn whether mankind still held him in high regard. Disguising himself as a commoner, he went into a sculptor's studio and examined the statues on display.

"How much for this statue of Jupiter?" Mercury asked.

"That's one of my inferior works," the sculptor replied. "You can have it for one drachma."

"How much for that statue of Juno over there in the corner?"

"That's one of my favorite works," said the sculptor. "My asking price is three drachmas."

The god then saw a statue of himself. Now, Mercury was the source of all important communiqués from the gods, so he thought his statue would command an exceptionally high price.

"What a beautiful piece of artwork!" he remarked. "How much for this statue of Mercury?"

"Friend," the sculptor replied with a smile, "I want to make you one of my loyal, long-term customers so I'm willing to make you a bargain. Pay me the prices I quoted you on the Jupiter and Juno statues, and I'll throw this one in for free."

{
AESOP'S MORAL:
*A person shopping for compliments
often comes away empty-handed.*
}

PERSPECTIVE: The smartest companies forge strong and lasting relationships with their customers. Who can fault the sculptor for trying to make Mercury a loyal patron? His mistake was innocent and understandable enough: not recognizing his disguised customer. What percentage of your company's sales is repeat business? How does your company attract and keep customers? How well do *you* know your customers? How do you stay close to your customers in the face of shifting market trends?

I tend to be a loyal customer. I've been going to the same barbershop for more than *forty years*. There are plenty of barbershops closer to my home, but I keep driving ten miles to this shop. Why? Nick, Dominic, and Rich know me personally. Their prices are reasonable, they greet me warmly at the door, and they know how I like my hair cut without having to say a word. (I can also get advice on any subject in the world at no extra charge: where to get the best cannoli in the city, how to train my dog, and the name of a good carpenter or electrician.) They make getting my hair cut an enjoyable experience instead of a chore. I wish every business I frequent knew me as well.

Keeping close to customers is a continuous process. Companies have traditionally used suggestion boxes, consumer surveys, and exit interviews to track what customers want, what product improvements need to be made, and how to provide better service. These approaches were fine in the past, but today there are more powerful ways to know your customers better, fueled in large part by computers.

I typically buy CDs online from Amazon.com. I like the fact that the company keeps track of my purchases and even offers suggestions for other artists I might like or alerts me when a new CD from a favorite artist is available. Amazon's computers know my tastes better than the local music shop at the mall. Computers give us the ability to know our customers and their preferences as never before. Ask

Microsoft's Bill Gates, who in his book *Business @ the Speed of Thought* describes how Jiffy Lube successfully uses its computer databases to get to know its customers better.

If you drive into a Jiffy Lube and ask for 10W-40 oil, the service technician will go to the computer and type in your vehicle's make and model to see what type of oil the manufacturer recommends. Going further, the technician can check the same records for vehicle specifications on oil filters, windshield wipers, transmission fluid, and grease. Each Jiffy Lube station can service forty-five cars per day because the process has been streamlined to avoid lines—they know how much you hate to wait! The number of technicians on duty is keyed to historical records on customer traffic patterns, so your wait is minimized. Three months after your visit, Jiffy Lube sends you a service reminder for your next oil change. The company keeps records of how many miles you drive between visits and develops insights into your driving habits and product preferences.

Gates describes how the customer assessments don't stop there: "The Jiffy Lube manager usually isn't an expert in market research, so headquarters employees do marketing and trend analysis. The information they use includes statistics, maps and profiles of . . . customers. The data show sales by different neighborhoods . . . including which neighborhoods might be ripe for a promotion."

If you've been bypassing a neighborhood Jiffy Lube for another one farther away, the computer system gives Jiffy Lube an opportunity to investigate why. Maybe your pattern is a result of natural traffic flow. Then again, maybe your pattern is a signal that there are problems at the closer store.

The company's information on its customers' preferences is enormous—each station has a database of 8,000 to 50,000 customers. Jiffy Lube is presently consolidating all of this information to make it possible for you to drive to any of its outlets in the United States and have your vehicle's service history readily available at that outlet.

{
BUSINESS MORAL:
Increase the potential for repeat business by knowing your customers as well as possible.
}

SOURCE

Gates, Bill. *Business @ the Speed of Thought,* 201–5. New York: Warner Books, 1999.

The Lioness

A loud noise in the forest turned out to be a group of animals in a raucous debate about which of them could produce the largest litter.

A mouse bragged, "I had eight babies at once! Try to beat that."

"That's nothing," a muskrat snickered. "I had ten babies in my litter."

A fox saw a lioness sitting quietly nearby and sneered: "How many cubs did *you* have in *your* litter?"

"Only one this time," she proudly replied, "but it's a lion!"

{
AESOP'S MORAL:
Quality is more important than quantity.
}

PERSPECTIVE: No leader set higher standards for himself than Joyce C. Hall, the man who built Hallmark Cards, claims Jack Mingo in *How the Cadillac Got Its Fins*. In 1910, Hall dropped out of high school to focus more time on his postcard distribution business. His brother eventually joined him, and they named their company Hall Brothers.

Business went well until 1915 when a warehouse fire destroyed all of the postcards that Hall had amassed in time for Valentine's Day. Because of that misfortune and devastating financial loss, Hall decided to start manufacturing his cards in addition to distributing them. The business boomed. Why? Hall Brothers cards were unique and well made. Customers liked sending quality cards, even though the sentiments inside them were a bit sticky sweet.

Hall changed the name of the company to Hallmark in 1954 to highlight the quality of his products and capitalize on his name. He came up with a slogan to promote his cards that thrives to this very day: "When you care enough to send the very best," which was another way to stress Hallmark's dedication to quality.

Hall thought that the new medium of television would be perfect for advertising his cards. He believed his company should focus on sponsoring quality programming just before Christmas, Valentine's Day, Mother's Day, and Easter—the biggest card-sending days of the year. I'm sure you've heard of the *Hallmark Hall of Fame* and probably have watched some of the programs over the years. The dramas, theater productions, and occasional operas are typically top-notch.

Hall wrote in his autobiography: "If a man goes into business with only the idea of making a lot of money, chances are he won't. But if he puts service and quality first, the money will take care of itself."

> { BUSINESS MORAL:
> *Great companies usually start
> with a quality product.* }

SOURCES

Hall, Joyce C. *When You Care Enough*, 240. Kansas City, MO: Hallmark, 1979.

Mingo, Jack. *How the Cadillac Got Its Fins*, 180–82. New York: HarperCollins, 1994.

The Stag at the Pool

A stag came to a pool of water in the woods on a hot summer's day. As the animal bent down to drink, he saw his reflection and couldn't help noticing how large and magnificent his antlers were.

My antlers make me different from most other creatures in the forest, the stag thought to himself. *Few animals are as handsomely adorned. I wish the rest of me was so well put together. These skinny legs and little hooves are no match for such a noble headpiece.*

As the stag stood admiring himself, an arrow zipped by his head. Immediately, the animal bounded away and found a safe haven in a dense thicket.

Once out of harm's way, though, the animal started craning his neck to get a better look at himself until his antlers got tangled in a tree. The more he struggled, the more ensnared he got. Hearing the thrashing, the hunter found the stag and put an arrow into him.

With his dying breath, the stag sighed, *I hated my legs that saved my life, and loved my antlers that were my ruin.*

{
AESOP'S MORAL:
*Few people appreciate the very
things that are most useful to them.*
}

PERSPECTIVE: What do you think differentiates your firm from the competition? Differentiation means offering your customers something that is unique and valuable above and beyond lower prices. In fact, successfully differentiated firms can demand premium prices for their products and services, and expect customer loyalty during business downturns.

A firm can differentiate itself in many ways, says Michael Porter in *Competitive Advantage*.[1] Scientists perceive Cray Research's super-computers as having superior technological capabilities. Perdue Chicken changed operations and began feeding its chickens marigolds to give them a more appealing color and differentiate its product from others in the supermarket. And FedEx developed an integrated logistical system that provided unheard-of reliability in small parcel delivery.

Firms can differentiate themselves anywhere along the product line. Think raw materials. Steinway chooses only the finest woods for its pianos. Michelin selects high-grade rubber for its tires.

Think distribution. Estee Lauder uses only select distribution outlets for its products. Caterpillar, Inc., has more dealers on average than other companies in its industry. This geographic coverage gives the company the ability to differentiate with outstanding service.

Think timing. Gerber was one of the first to co-opt the image of baby food provider. Bausch and Lomb was one of the first companies to receive regulatory approval for its soft contact lenses.

Think prestige. People buy Rolex watches, Gulfstream jets, and Corvettes because they want the images these products convey.

Does your firm have a differentiation strategy? If not, Porter offers eight steps to help you develop one:

1. *Determine who the real buyer is*. Firms, institutions, and households don't buy your products—people do. Talk to them, and find out exactly what they value.

2. *Identify the customer's value chain*. Help your customers lower their costs or raise their performance. Examine their buying channels.

3. *Determine purchasing criteria priorities*. Is it utility? Then create value. Is the value already there? Then help your customers uncover it.

4. *Assess potential sources in the value chain for uniqueness*. Look at procurement, human resources, raw materials, operations, marketing, sales, and service.

5. *Determine the costs of differentiation*. Differentiated firms deliberately invest more in certain activities to become unique.

6. *Choose those activities that provide the most value*. It's likely that your company may have to alter more than one of its activities to create that value.

7. *Test the differentiation for sustainability*. Can competitors easily imitate your lead? Do customers perceive the value to be long-lasting? If not, the differentiation isn't sustainable.

8. *Reduce costs in activities not associated with the differentiation*. If there are facets of your product that customers don't value, aggressively cut costs in those areas.

Make no mistake: differentiation is hard, and sustaining it even harder. But the company that understands the facets of its products and services valued most by its customers is the one least likely to end up like the stag.

{ **BUSINESS MORAL:**
Help your company become unique at something that your customers truly value. }

The Donkey *and* His Purchaser

A man went to the market to buy a donkey to add to his stable. When he saw one he wanted to buy, he said to the owner: "Let me take him home to test him out. If I like the way he works, I'll come back and pay you for him."

The owner agreed to the arrangement, so the man took the donkey home and put him in the stable. The animal looked around at the other donkeys and then lay down next to the laziest one.

"Just as I suspected," the man said. He grabbed a halter and took the donkey back to the owner.

"What's wrong?" the surprised owner asked. "You couldn't possibly have tested the animal so quickly."

"One small test was enough for me," said the man. "I could tell what kind of worker he was just by the companion he chose for himself."

{
AESOP'S MORAL:
You are judged by the company you keep.
}

PERSPECTIVE: As consumers, most of us like to try something out or on before buying it. We wouldn't think of purchasing a car before taking it for a test-drive or buying clothes before trying them on. Advertisers ask us to "take advantage of our thirty-day trial offer," or they tell us to "*try* it, you'll like it." Just today, I taste-tested a new brand of cheddar cheese at the supermarket, listened to portions of

172

a CD online to see if it was worth buying, and received a free one-month subscription to a local newspaper.

The best companies also make it a point to conduct trial runs and test markets. Why? These methods reduce a company's risk of failure. The most successful companies make strident efforts to experiment with new products or services in test markets before unveiling them on a wide scale, assert Thomas Peters and Robert Waterman Jr. in their book *In Search of Excellence*. More and more, though, it seems companies are testing less and less: "Our experience has been that most institutions have forgotten how to test and learn. They seem to prefer analysis and debate to trying something out, and they are paralyzed by fear of failure, however small."

McDonald's is known for test-marketing new menu items. Testing helped the company make its hugely successful expansion into breakfast items years ago. Ore-Ida Company constantly undertakes taste tests, marketing tests, and pricing tests for its products. Hewlett-Packard, 3M, Holiday Inn, and Procter & Gamble (P&G) consistently test and experiment. In fact, the authors quote an executive from Crown Zellerbach, a P&G competitor: "P&G tests and tests and tests. You can see them coming for months, often years. But you know when they get there, it is probably time for you to move on to another niche, not to be in their way. They leave no stone unturned, no variable untested."

What happens when an organization doesn't test enough? The picture isn't pretty. Look no farther than the National Aeronautics and Space Administration (NASA). NASA implemented an approach called Success Oriented Management to control space shuttle development that basically assumed everything would go right. How realistic is that in the face of Murphy's Law, which says whatever can go wrong will go wrong?

According to Peters and Waterman, this approach—which mini-mized testing and maximized finger crossing—led to "wholesale defer-rals of difficult work, embarrassing accidents, expensive redesigns, erratic staffing, and the illusion that everything is running well." Five major fires resulted when NASA used the technique to develop the space shuttle's engines. Is it any wonder that people question whether the *Challenger* and *Columbia* tragedies could have been avoided had NASA better tested O-ring performance in cold weather or the poten-tial for structural damage to the shuttle body from insulation foam breaking away during liftoff?

Testing alone won't prevent failure, though; companies have to conduct the *right* tests. Coca-Cola was sure its New Coke was going to be a success—extensive testing told the management so. In an unprecedented move, Coca-Cola decided to tamper with its flagship recipe to fend off Pepsi's relentless increases in market share. In fact, it looked like Pepsi was about to surpass Coca-Cola in total sales for the first time ever. In numerous taste tests, people said they liked New Coke better than Pepsi or even the original Coke, by an overwhelm-ing margin. It tasted smoother and sweeter than original Coke, a taste that was more like Pepsi. The confident company stopped production of the original Coke and launched New Coke on April 23, 1985.

It was a colossal failure. Consumers seemed to hate the taste of the new product. What went wrong? The company didn't ask the right questions during the taste tests. If designers of the test had asked the subjects how they felt about the new cola *replacing* the old one, they would have been overwhelmed at the loyalty the subjects felt for the original formula. Consumer loyalty was a much stronger motivator to buy than subjective changes in sweetness or flavor. People felt betrayed by the switch. The new product never had a chance.

How serious is your organization about testing new products or services, either ones you're selling or ones you're buying? How do you know whether you're testing enough? How do you know whether you're making the right tests and asking the right questions? What failures have you had that might have been avoided with a little more testing? The next time you or your company is thinking about doing something new, follow the advice of the man buying the donkey: when in doubt, try it out.

{
BUSINESS MORAL:
The right little tests can prevent great failures.
}

SOURCE

Peters, Thomas J., and Robert H. Waterman Jr. *In Search of Excellence: Lessons from America's Best-Run Companies,* 135–37, 143. New York: Harper and Row, 1982.

Negotiations, Mergers, *and* Alliances

---

*If you have integrity, nothing else matters. If you
don't have integrity, nothing else matters.*

—ALAN SIMPSON
(THREE-TERM U.S. SENATOR, R-WYOMING, 1931–)

*Keep a guard upon your words as well as your
actions, that there be no impurity in either.*

—AESOP

The Lion, the Donkey, *and* the Fox

A lion, a donkey, and a fox decided to form a hunting party. They tracked, caught, and killed an enormous stag.

The lion said to the donkey: "Divide up the spoils so we can eat. I'm hungry."

The donkey divided the stag into three equal portions. When the lion saw the portions, he roared angrily, pounced on the donkey, and killed him.

Looking at the fox, the lion said, "Now it's your turn. Divide the stag into two parts."

The fox looked over at the mauled carcass of the donkey, took a small mouthful of meat, and pushed the remaining pieces of the stag toward the king of beasts.

The lion nodded in approval and asked, "Who taught you to negotiate so well?"

The fox glanced again at the dead donkey and replied, "Why, my belated friend over there taught me everything I know."

{
AESOP'S MORAL:
We can learn by the misfortunes of others.
}

PERSPECTIVE: What have you negotiated recently? A pay raise? The price of a new house or a used car? What rules do you follow when you negotiate? Based on your experience, what mistakes did the donkey make in negotiating a "fair" split of the spoils?

Bob Woolf was a master negotiator who represented many prominent celebrities during his lifetime and negotiated with numerous business figures, including Red Auerbach, Ted Turner, and Donald Trump. In *Friendly Persuasion*, Woolf explained more than fifty rules for negotiating. I think some of his most important ones include:

- Make sure the person across the table has the authority to sign off on the deal.

- Create a good atmosphere.

- Dress for respect.

- Lose your ego, be self-effacing, and don't take anything personally.

- Deal in good faith. Have the attitude: "I'm going to make a deal today."

- Do your homework.

- Realize that almost everything is negotiable.

- Keep the word *demand* out of your vocabulary, and never issue ultimatums.

- Constantly reassess your leverage.

- Keep a record of each negotiating session.

- Don't negotiate when you're tired.

Woolf had one other important rule, and it's the one the donkey broke. In fact, Brian Epstein, the Beatles' manager, broke the same rule.

The year was 1963, and the Beatles were beginning to make a big splash. A movie producer approached Epstein about making a film featuring the Fab Four. United Artists was prepared to financially back the film. Movie company executives offered the Beatles $25,000 to appear in the film plus an unspecified percentage of the profits. They asked Epstein to tell them what he wanted as the percentage

Epstein had no experience in moviemaking—most of his experience came out of the retail furniture business. Epstein made minimal effort to research what an equitable percentage would be for a low-budget film with only modest expectations of success. "I wouldn't accept anything less than 7.5 percent," Epstein is reported to have said.

Big mistake. "Get the other side to make the first offer," Woolf advised. "Not only did he make the mistake of going first with his proposal . . . he was misinformed as to the norm of getting paid higher percentages of a profit when the movie's low budget prevented higher cash advances to the talent."

In fact, the movie executives were prepared to offer up to *25 percent* of the profits. The movie, *A Hard Day's Night,* grossed many millions of dollars. And while the Beatles made lots of money on music sales, they missed an opportunity to make still more money on the film.

{
BUSINESS MORAL:
When you sit down to negotiate, be prepared, be patient, and be all ears.
}

SOURCE
Woolf, Bob. *Friendly Persuasion: My Life as a Negotiator,* 180. New York: Putnam, 1990.

The Fox *and* the Goat

A fox accidentally fell into a well. He tried to climb the high walls, but they were too slippery. As the fox treaded water at the bottom, a thirsty goat came to the top of the well.

"What happened to you?" the goat asked.

"Maybe you haven't heard the news," replied the fox, "but a great drought is under way. I jumped down here to get as much water as I could. You should do the same thing before all the water is gone."

The goat hesitated. "Are you sure there's a drought?" she asked.

"Look around you," said the fox. "Don't the leaves on the trees look slightly browner and the grass a bit wilted? Better to be down here with all this water—I drank so much, my belly is ready to burst."

Looking around at the trees and bushes, the goat decided they *did* look a little brown, so she jumped into the well. As soon as the goat hit the bottom of the well, the fox jumped on her back and scrambled out to safety.

As he ran away, the fox shouted back to the goat: "It's better to look before you leap!"

{ AESOP'S MORAL:
*Don't trust the advice
of someone in distress.* }

PERSPECTIVE: Perception is reality in the mind of the perceiver. A thousand years ago, people perceived the sun moving across the sky and concluded the sun revolved around the earth. Madison Avenue makes a living by creating false perceptions: drink this beer, and women will flock to you; buy this car, and you'll make your life complete. Something in our human nature makes us want to buy into these illusions even though we know they're patently false.

Companies are not immune to buying into false perceptions either. Every business deal has one or two inherent illusions. Nothing is *exactly* what it seems. Ask Donald Trump. In *The Art of the Deal*, he describes creating an illusion that allowed him to close a huge deal on one of his Atlantic City casinos.

Trump Plaza Corporation had received its license from the New Jersey Casino Control Commission. All of the architectural and building plans had been approved. The immediate problem became execution: Trump had extensive experience in constructing buildings, but none in operating a casino. At that point, Michael Rose, chairman of Holiday Inn, approached Trump with a partnering deal: Trump would build the casino, Holiday Inn would operate it, and they would split the profits fifty-fifty. Even better, Holiday Inn had the financial resources to finance the deal, so Trump wouldn't need to use any of his money. As far as Trump was concerned, there was no downside to the arrangement. Negotiations were completed. The only remaining point was for the Holiday Inn board of directors to approve the deal. That's when things got a bit tricky.

Holiday Inn deliberately scheduled its annual board of directors meeting in Atlantic City so that the members could view what Trump had called the "best site on the Boardwalk" and, more important, assess construction progress. The problem was that little progress had been made on the site, thereby possibly jeopardizing or delaying the deal. Trump had one week to address the problem.

"I called in my construction supervisor," explained Trump, "and told him that I wanted him to round up every bulldozer and dump truck he could possibly find." The equipment operators were told to make the almost vacant two-acre parcel look like the "most active construction site in the history of the world." Dump trucks moved dirt back and forth across the site; bulldozers dug holes and later refilled them. The perception was that an amazing amount of activity was taking place, though the truth was that nothing was really happening.

The Holiday Inn board of directors toured the site the next week, and many were awed by the level of activity on the property. "You know," one member remarked to Trump, "it's great when you are a private guy, and you can pull out all the stops." The board members returned home, completely assured. Three weeks later, they signed the partnership agreement, and Trump was in the casino business.

{
BUSINESS MORAL:
Do your best to uncover the illusions that exist in every business deal.
}

SOURCE

Trump, Donald. *The Art of the Deal,* 141–43. New York: Random House, 1988.

The Lion in Love

Long ago, a lion fell in love with a woodsman's daughter. Mesmerized by her beauty, the lion approached the woodsman to ask for the maiden's hand in marriage. The woodsman was entirely against the arrangement but feared the displeasure of the royal beast should he refuse to consent.

"Your Majesty and King of the Forest," the woodsman said, "my wife and I are flattered by your proposal but fear some harm could inadvertently befall our young daughter when you are expressing your affection for her. If you'd consent to having your claws removed and your teeth extracted, we'd consent to making you her bridegroom."

The lion was so deeply in love that he had his claws and teeth removed. But when he returned to claim the maiden, the woodsman, no longer afraid of the harmless beast, grabbed a thick club and drove the groom-to-be back into the woods.

AESOP'S MORAL:
The overeager make bad decisions.

PERSPECTIVE: This story is about negotiation, not love. The lion's intense desire to make the maiden his bride clouded his thinking and made him vulnerable to the woodsman's outrageous conditions. In *You Can Negotiate Anything,* Herb Cohen cautions about being too eager to enter a deal. He identifies three crucial variables in negotiating: leveraging power, information, and time.

The woodsman held the leveraging power in this instance because the lion was love struck and wanted something that the woodsman didn't want to give up. Had the lion noted all of the key information available, especially the woodsman's trembling legs, he would have realized he could have threatened the woodsman and his wife with their lives. The lion also wanted to complete the marriage arrangement as soon as possible—making time a critical factor. The woodsman could have waited endlessly since he didn't want to make the deal.

"Care about the deal," Cohen advises, "but never that much." He cites the example of the United States eagerly wanting to end the Vietnam War.

When North Vietnam agreed to hold peace talks in Paris, the U.S. immediately sent Averell Harriman as its chief negotiator. He rented a room at the Place Vendome in the middle of the city—on a *week-to-week* basis. In contrast, the North Vietnamese took out a *two-and-a-half-year lease* on a villa *outside* Paris. Obviously, they believed that time was on their side given antiwar sentiments in the U.S., and there was no need to come to terms immediately.

The delaying tactics of the North Vietnamese started before they even sat down. Negotiators began arguing about nameplates, the order the countries would speak in, and—in one of the most inane developments—the shape of the negotiating table. The North Vietnamese wanted a four-sided table to emphasize equality among the parties. The U.S. preferred a two-sided table.

The war and the negotiations dragged on. Time pressures forced the U.S. into concessions it would have preferred to avoid. Did North Vietnam's nonchalance and dawdling affect the negotiations?

"Emphatically it did," says Cohen. "In retrospect, we can now understand why the Paris peace accords never successfully resolved the war—at least, to our satisfaction."

{
BUSINESS MORAL:
When negotiating, never be too eager to come to terms—true negotiating power comes from being able to walk away at any time.
}

SOURCE

Cohen, Herb. *You Can Negotiate Anything—How to Get What You Really Want*, 95–96. Secaucus, NJ: L. Stuart, 1980.

The Porcupine *and* the Snakes

A porcupine searched the woods for a place to house his small family during the winter. He finally came across a small, comfortable cave. The porcupine was thrilled at finding the winter quarters until he went into the cave and saw a family of snakes already living there.

"Would it be okay if my family and I used a small part of your cave to spend the winter?" the porcupine asked.

The snakes had reservations about sharing their home, but eventually agreed to let the porcupines in. It wasn't long, though, before the snakes realized that they'd made a big mistake. Every time a snake moved, he pricked himself on one of the visitors' quills.

After bearing this discomfort for a few days, the snakes finally complained. "This isn't going to work," the head of the snake family hissed. "Your quills are making it impossible for us to sleep."

"That's too bad," yawned the drowsy father porcupine. "We're very comfortable here. If you snakes aren't happy, why don't you go somewhere else?"

He then curled himself into a ball and went back to sleep.

{
AESOP'S MORAL:
Make sure you know your guests before offering them hospitality.
}

PERSPECTIVE: Mergers are tricky business. You might have guessed that a merger between porcupines and snakes, or lions and lambs, or foxes and chickens for that matter, might not succeed, no matter how cordial the honeymoon. How many business mergers begin with good intentions, yet end badly? Too many, says Robert Heller in *The Naked Manager*. "Most mergers are created in pious hope; their guiding drive is not financial or industrial logic but, in various forms, the urge to aggrandize."

Heller lists some reasons why these "friendly" mergers often don't work. The senior partners are too nice and pay too much for a company, thereby negating any financial bonanza. Nobody's job is redundant. Every product or service is essential. Nothing changes. The result? The merger achieves zero synergy. In many cases, the buyer knows nothing about the business it just acquired. How can senior managers evaluate performance when they know nothing about the industry?

Some of the worst mergers have been of this know-nothing nature. Two oil companies, Sohio and Atlantic Ritchfield, bought copper companies, which resulted in each decreasing earnings by about 20 percent. Exxon bought into electrical equipment and utterly wasted $1.24 billion doing it. Mobil bought Montgomery Ward stores—a move that knocked 40 percent off earnings that year.

The marriage of Time Warner and AOL has been called one of the most calamitous mergers in history. In 2000, the merger looked like a great idea. Time Warner CEO Jerry Levin believed that linking up with the darling of the Internet would infuse his rock-ribbed conglomerate with a new spirit and cachet. AOL's Steve Case liked the idea that his company would gain access to enormous entertainment content. When the Internet bubble burst, AOL proved to be an extremely fragile partner. In January 2000, AOL Time Warner had a combined market capitalization of $280 billion. By February 2003, it was only $49 billion. AOL Time Warner lost $100 billion in 2002 alone. On September 17, 2003, the company announced it was changing its name back to Time Warner.

What about mergers between companies engaged in the same business? Unfortunately, other issues can put a marriage between kindred companies on the rocks. Consider Mary Wells Lawrence's story.

Mary is one of advertising's all-time superstars. Remember Alka-Seltzer's "Plop plop fizz fizz" slogan? That's hers. She also convinced Braniff Airways to paint its aircraft with vivid colors. She developed the "Midasized" Midas Muffler, Ford's "Quality Is Job One," and the "I Love New York" ad campaigns. Mary started her own advertising firm, Wells Rich Greene, Inc., in 1966. When she took her firm public, she became the first woman CEO of a company on the New York Stock Exchange.

In 1990, a French advertising firm called BDDP approached Mary about merging with her company to capitalize on the globalization then taking place in the advertising industry. A merger made sense at that time, and everyone believed it would foster an international synergy. On April 12, 1990, Mary presented the new company, called Wells BDDP, to the advertising world. Everyone was all smiles at the New York press conference. It wouldn't be long, though, before the smiles turned to grimaces and the principals began reaching for the Alka-Seltzer tablets.

For the merger to work, BDDP's executives had to spend a lot of time in New York. They didn't. The families of key executives didn't want to move. On top of that, the French are notoriously disinterested tourists. "I read once where the French people go on Zoloft for separation anxiety when they leave the country," Mary joked. The management at Wells Rich Greene soon realized that BDDP's executives were buyers, not doers. The merger stagnated. Clients questioned the new firm's identity and then began leaving in droves.

Ron Moore, the chairman of Midas, one of Mary's good clients, told the press that after the merger, "we increasingly saw a highly driven service organization with a personal touch become a highly commercial financial concern."

The agency's future began circling the drain. Beginning in 1995, Wells BDDP lost almost a half billion dollars in billings. It closed its doors in May 1998.

{
BUSINESS MORAL:
Friendly mergers usually don't benefit the stockholders in the long run.
}

SOURCES

Heller, Robert. *The Naked Manager: Games Executives Play,* 115, 119, 123. New York: T. Talley Books, 1985.

Lawrence, Mary Wells. *A Big Life (in Advertising),* 284-89. New York: Knopf, 2002.

The Lion *and* the Dolphin

The king of the jungle was walking along the seashore one day and saw a dolphin breaking the surface of the water.

"Brother Dolphin," said the lion, "how fortuitous that we should meet! I'm king of the jungle and you're king of the fish. It makes perfect sense to me that we join forces, become allies, and rule earth and water."

"Your proposal makes a lot of sense," the dolphin replied. "Let's become partners."

Not long after, the lion was again walking along the shore when a wild bull challenged him. The bull turned out to be a fierce fighter and pinned down the king of beasts. The lion called to the dolphin for help. The dolphin heard the lion's cry and earnestly wanted to join the battle, but couldn't leave the sea. Eventually, the lion prevailed, and the wild bull fled into the woods.

At that point, the lion began to scold the dolphin: "A fine ally you turned out to be. I could have been killed. You didn't do anything to help me."

"Don't blame me," said the dolphin. "Instead, blame nature, which made me swift and mighty in the sea but useless on land."

{
AESOP'S MORAL:
When choosing allies, consider their abilities as well as their willingness to help.
}

PERSPECTIVE: All of us can use a good ally. In the office, mentors and friends in high places can help our careers. On a larger scale, alliances between companies can create synergies that benefit both organizations.

Who are your personal allies at work? How have they helped you in the past? Has your company ever hooked up with another company in a business venture? How did it work out?

There are many issues to consider when forming strategic alliances: company size, financial health, relative market share, cultural compatibility, shared goals, shared commitment, and geographic coverage. The world is filled with stories of peoples, companies, and governments forming partnerships and alliances that altered the course of history. Look at us! The colonies were able to become an independent country, in part, because of a shrewd alliance the Founding Fathers made during the Revolutionary War. According to Don Phillips in *The Founding Fathers on Leadership,* America's leaders knew it was important to build long-term strategic alliances with foreign countries to have any chance of defeating the British.

Hostilities broke out between the colonists and British soldiers at Lexington, Massachusetts on April 18, 1775. After the Declaration of Independence was signed on July 4, 1776, there was no turning back. To defeat the British, the colonists realized they would need help from foreign governments. After considering all of the European countries, the U.S. decided that the key to victory was getting France involved in the war, and thus dispatched Benjamin Franklin to Paris in December 1776. Franklin relentlessly went about his diplomatic mission with King Louis XVI to make France an ally. On February 6, 1778, the U.S. and France signed the Treaty of Alliance; the patriots' defeat of the British at the First and Second Battles at Freeman's Farm, New York, convinced France that, with help, the U.S. could win the war.

The alliance greatly helped both parties. The colonists welcomed thousands of French troops previously stationed in the West Indies, troops who were well equipped and experienced from a recent war against the British. France's formidable naval force bolstered Washington's meager navy. England, upon hearing of the treaty, found itself potentially fighting a world war instead of suppressing a family dispute. Consequently, England began to dilute its army and navy to cover more territory to protect itself. Major antiwar factions arose in England, undermining the resolve of the government.

For its part, France dramatically increased its trade and market opportunities with the colonies, and other European countries were forced to choose sides. Wanting access to the new nation's goods, many countries, like Spain, sided against England. Three years later, in October 1781, Lord Cornwallis surrendered to General George Washington at Yorktown, Virginia, in the war's last major battle.

Phillips provides a final word: "In essence, building strong alliances—whether with individuals or groups—allows leaders to achieve more results for themselves and for their organizations."

{
BUSINESS MORAL:
Form alliances with capable partners
who share the same key goals.
}

SOURCE
Phillips, Donald T. *The Founding Fathers on Leadership: Classic Teamwork in Changing Times,* 141, 147–49. New York: Warner Books, 1997.

About the Author

David Noonan has been a consultant to industry and government for more than twenty-five years. He has helped address the environmental compliance, health, and safety issues for many clients including American Stores Properties Inc., Digital Equipment Corporation, Lucent Technologies, Merck Pharmaceutical, Uno Restaurant Corporation, the Environmental Protection Agency, the Federal Emergency Management Agency, and the Department of Defense. He received his BS in engineering from Northeastern University and his MBA from the University of Southern New Hampshire. He has coauthored two engineering textbooks and more than three dozen professional papers and has been a guest lecturer at the Massachusetts Institute of Technology and Northeastern University. He lives with his wife and family in Hanover, Massachusetts.

Bibliography

Abrashoff, Captain D. Michael. *It's Your Ship: Management Techniques from the Best Damn Ship in the Navy*. New York: Warner Books, 2002.

Aesop's Fables. Mahwah, NJ: Watermill Press, 1985.

Aurandt, Paul. *Paul Harvey's The Rest of the Story*. Edited and compiled by Lynne Harvey. Garden City, NY: Doubleday, 1977.

Bennis, Warren G. *On Becoming a Leader*. Reading, MA: Addison-Wesley Publishing Company, 1989.

Bossidy, Larry, and Ram Charan. *Execution: The Discipline of Getting Things Done*. New York: Crown Business, 2002.

Bruzzese, Anita. *Take This Job and Thrive: 60 Ways to Make Life More Rewarding in Today's Workplace*. Manassas Park, VA: Impact Publications, 2000.

Carey, Benedict. "Fear in the Workplace: The Bullying Boss." *New York Times*, June 22, 2004.

Carnegie, Dale. *How to Win Friends and Influence People*. New York: Simon and Schuster, 1964.

Clifford, Donald K., Jr., and Richard E. Cavanagh. *The Winning Performance: How America's High-Growth Midsize Companies Succeed*. New York: Bantam Books, 1985.

Cohen, Herb. *You Can Negotiate Anything—How to Get What You Really Want*. Secaucus, NJ: L. Stuart, 1980.

Collins, James C., and Jerry I. Porras. *Built to Last: Successful Habits of Visionary Companies*. New York: HarperBusiness, 1994.

Coulson, Robert. *The Termination Handbook*. New York: Free Press, 1981.

Covey, Stephen R. *The 7 Habits of Highly Effective People*. New York: Simon and Schuster, 1998.

Deming, W. Edwards. *Out of the Crisis*. Cambridge, MA: Massachusetts Institute of Technology, Center for Advanced Engineering Study, 1986.

Dixit, Avinash, and Barry Nalebuff. *Thinking Strategically: The Competitive Edge in Business, Politics and Everyday Life*. New York: W. W. Norton and Company, 1993.

Drucker, Peter F. *The Essential Drucker*. New York: HarperCollins, 2001.

————. *Managing in Turbulent Times*. New York: HarperBusiness, 1993.

Fassel, Diane. *Working Ourselves to Death: The High Cost of Workaholism and the Rewards of Recovery*. San Francisco, CA: HarperCollins, 1990.

Fields, Debbi, with Alan Furst. *One Smart Cookie*. New York: Simon and Schuster, 1987.

Freeman, Dr. Arthur M., and Rose DeWolf. *The 10 Dumbest Mistakes Smart People Make and How to Avoid Them*. New York: HarperCollins, 1992.

Gates, Bill. *Business @ the Speed of Thought*. New York: Warner Books, 1999.

Giuliani, Rudolph W. *Leadership*. New York: Hyperion, 2002.

Greene, Robert, and Joost Elffers. *The 48 Laws of Power*. New York: Viking, 1998.

Half, Robert. *On Hiring*. New York: Crown Publishers, 1985.

Hall, Joyce C. *When You Care Enough*. Kansas City, MO: Hallmark, 1979.

Harari, Oren. *The Leadership Secrets of Colin Powell*. New York: McGraw-Hill, 2002.

Hayes, Dennis. *Behind the Silicon Curtain: The Seductions of Work in a Lonely Era*. Boston, MA: South End Press, 1989.

Heller, Robert. *The Naked Manager: Games Executives Play*. New York: T. Talley Books, 1985.

Hill, Napoleon. *Napoleon Hill's Keys to Success: The 17 Principles of Personal Achievement*. New York: Dutton, 1994.

Iacocca, Lee. *Iacocca: An Autobiography*. New York: Bantam Books, 1984.

James, Geoffrey. *Business Wisdom of the Electronic Elite: 34 Winning Management Strategies from CEOs at Microsoft, Compaq, Sun, Hewlett-Packard, and Other Top Companies*. New York: Times Business/Random House, 1996.

Kaltman, Al. *Cigars, Whiskey and Winning: Leadership Lessons from General Ulysses S. Grant*. Paramus, NJ: Prentice Hall Press, 1998.

Kanter, Rosabeth Moss, et al. *Innovation: Breakthrough Thinking at 3M, DuPont, GE, Pfizer, and Rubbermaid*. New York: HarperBusiness, 1997.

Kawasaki, Guy. *How to Drive Your Competition Crazy: Creating Disruption for Fun and Profit*. New York: Hyperion, 1995.

Kelley, Robert Earl. *How to Be a Star at Work: Nine Breakthrough Strategies You Need to Succeed*. New York: Times Business, 1998.

Kingsley, Daniel. *How to Fire an Employee: An Essential Guide to Humane, Fair, and Effective Techniques for All Responsible Business People*. New York: Facts on File, 1984.

Koehn, Nancy F. *Brand New: How Entrepreneurs Earned Customers' Trust from Wedgwood to Dell*. Boston, MA: Harvard Business School Press, 2001.

Krzyzewski, Mike. *Leading with the Heart: Coach K's Successful Strategies for Basketball, Business and Life*. New York: Warner Books, 2000.

Lauder, Estee. *Estee: A Success Story*. New York: Random House, 1985.

Lawrence, Mary Wells. *A Big Life (in Advertising)*. New York: Knopf, 2002.

Levinson, Jay C., and Seth Godin. *The Guerrilla Marketing Handbook*. Boston, MA: Houghton Mifflin, 1994.

Lowe, Janet. *Oprah Winfrey Speaks: Insight from the World's Most Influential Voice*. New York: John Wiley & Sons, 1998.

Magretta, Joan. *What Management Is, How It Works, and Why It's Everyone's Business*. New York: Free Press, 2002.

Mayer, Gloria Gilbert, and Thomas Mayer. *Goldilocks on Management: 27 Revisionist Fairy Tales for Serious Managers*. New York: AMACOM, 1999.

McKenna, Patrick J., and David Maister. *First Among Equals: How to Manage a Group of Professionals*. New York: The Free Press, 2002.

Merwin, John. "The Sad Case of the Dwindling Orange Roofs." *Forbes*, December 30, 1985.

Mingo, Jack. *How the Cadillac Got Its Fins*. New York: HarperCollins, 1994.

Nelson, Bob. *1001 Ways to Reward Employees*. New York: Workman Publishers, 1994.

Nelson, Robert B. *Delegation: The Power of Letting Go*. Glenview, IL: Scott Foresman and Company, 1988.

Noonan, Peggy. *What I Saw at the Revolution*. New York: Random House, 1990.

O'Brien, Virginia. *Success on Our Own Terms: Tales of Extraordinary, Ordinary Business Women*. New York: John Wiley & Sons, 1998.

O'Shea, James, and Charles Madigan. *Dangerous Companies: The Consulting Powerhouses and the Businesses They Save and Ruin*. New York: Random House, Times Business, 1997.

Peters, Thomas J., and Robert H. Waterman Jr. *In Search of Excellence: Lessons from America's Best-Run Companies*. New York: Harper and Row, 1982.

Pfeffer, Jeffrey. *Competitive Advantage Through People: Unleashing the Power of the Work Force*. Boston, MA: Harvard Business School Press, 1994.

Phillips, Donald T. *The Founding Fathers on Leadership: Classic Teamwork in Changing Times*. New York: Warner Books, 1997.

Pitino, Rick. *Success Is a Choice: Ten Steps to Overachieving in Business and Life*. New York: Broadway Books, 1997.

Pollard, C. William. *The Soul of the Firm*. New York: HarperBusiness; Grand Rapids, MI: Zondervan Publishing House, 1996.

Porter, Michael E. *Competitive Advantage: Creating and Sustaining Superior Performance*. New York: The Free Press; London: Collier Macmillan, 1985.

Redstone, Sumner. "What I've Learned." *Esquire,* January 2003.

Reich, Robert. "The Moral Basis of Our Labor." *Boston Globe,* September 2, 1996.

Ridge, Warren J. *Follow Me! Business Leadership Patton Style*. New York: AMACOM, 1989.

Ross, Gerald, and Michael Kay. *Toppling the Pyramids: Redefining the Ways Companies Are Run*. New York: Times Books, 1994.

Seifter, Harvey. *Leadership Ensemble: Lessons in Collaborative Management from the World's Only Conductorless Orchestra*. New York: Times Books, 2001.

Sloan, Alfred P. *My Years with General Motors*. New York: Doubleday/Currency, 1963.

Torre, Joe. *Joe Torre's Ground Rules for Winners: 12 Keys to Managing Team Players, Tough Bosses, Setbacks and Success*. New York: Hyperion, 1999.

Trump, Donald. *The Art of the Deal*. New York: Random House, 1988.

Walton, Sam. *Sam Walton: Made in America*. New York: Doubleday, 1992.

Welch, Jack. *Jack: Straight from the Gut*. New York: Warner Books, 2001.

Woolf, Bob. *Friendly Persuasion: My Life as a Negotiator*. New York: Putnam, 1990.

U.S. Department of Labor. *Employment Characteristics and Families Summary*, USDL 04-719, April 20, 2004.